What a
Modern Catholic
Believes About

UPDATING

THEOLOGY

Part One
by George Malone

the thomas more press
chicago illinois

Standard Book Number: 0–88347–030–6

TABLE OF CONTENTS

Introduction

THE EVOLUTION OF
ROMAN CATHOLIC TEACHING

C HANGE is very much a part of our lives. Yet it is very true that we are always confused by change. For the past thirty years there have been unprecedented changes in all of our lives, changes occurring ever more rapidly and at an ever accelerating pace. Whole books have been written about this phenomenon of accelerating change, such as Don Fabun's *The Dynamics of Change* and Alvin Toffler's best seller, *Future Shock*.

It is not surprising that these changes have also affected the churches and theology. It is the purpose of these two volumes to investigate these changes, especially in relation to Roman Catholic church teaching and theology. We have attempted to present them objectively—that is, simply as statements of fact without any editorial bias, either conservative or liberal.

To set these changes in context, let us look first at the phenomenon of change in general and then at the implications of such change for theology and for church teachings.

THE FACT OF TECHNOLOGICAL CHANGE

In our daily lives we have seen many examples of such change. For example, the electric fan has given way to the air conditioner, the ice box to the refrigerator, the wood-burning stove to the gas and electric range. In two areas especially, change is most dramatically illustrated—the areas of transportation and communication.

In a short period of time we have advanced from mules and horses drawing stagecoaches to the steam engine with locomotives and trains. From automobiles, trucks and airplanes we have moved to jet planes and from jet planes to rocket launchings. In a certain sense one can now say that it is perhaps less difficult to go from the earth to the moon than from one part of the country to another.

The area of communication also shows striking advances. From letters written by hand and delivered by mail we have progressed to telephone and telegraph, from there to radio and television.

Today with satellites circling the earth and laser beams, instant communication anywhere in the world and even from outer space is a possibility. It is indeed difficult for us to realize that for hundreds of thousands of years man did not even have a printed, formal alphabet. Man has enjoyed an alphabet for only the past three or four thousand years.

It has been only within the past five hundred years that man has enjoyed the advantages of printing. Printing, in turn, gave man the opportunity to index information which he had written down. The growth of printing in itself is a remarkable phenomenon. Thirty years ago a scholar, a theologian, could read twenty-five or thirty journals and consider himself well up-to-date in his field. Today the number of such journals is approaching the level of one thousand. Looking at publication in general, we might estimate that each and every day five hundred thousand new pages of information are added to man's store of learning and reflection about himself, about God, and about the universe. How can one begin to cope with such a fantastic proliferation of writing?

THE FACT OF PHILOSOPHICAL CHANGE

The changes in our lives have been not only technological, but also philosophical. The many books of the Bible, from both the Old and New Testaments, are relatively unsophisticated philosophically. Unlike the Greeks, the ancient Hebrews did not indulge in abstract philosophical reasoning to any great extent. But as the young Christian community spread throughout the Mediterranean area there was bound to be a meeting, a confrontation with Greek philosophical thought.

The most striking instance of reflection in the early church about this area was that of St. Justin Martyr. Justin felt that there need be no conflict between pagan Greek philosophy and the message of the Christian gospel. Justin rightly felt that whatever had been rightly, truly, and beautifully said in pagan philosophy could and must be accommodated and adapted to Christian gospel preaching.

So it was that two philosophical schools came to exercise a great influence on the preaching of the Christian message. The first was the school of Platonic philosophy which found its epitome in the writings of St. Augustine, Bishop of Hippo. This Platonic emphasis on philosophy was the dominant philosophical school from the fourth to the thirteenth centuries. The second major current of philosophical reflection influencing Christian thought was the Aristotelian, which found its epitome in the *Summa Theologica* and further writings of St. Thomas Aquinas.

The dominant interest of Platonic philosophy was spiritual and idealistic. The dominant theme of Aristotelian philosophy was not materialistic but rather realistic. However, in both schools of philosophy there was a relatively static concept of nature, of essence, and of substance. To the question, "What is Man?" the answer was given, "Man is a rational animal." Having given this answer, one had given back man's essence, man's substance. Everything else over, above and beyond this was considered to be accidental. Thus it was that there was a great emphasis upon essences which were considered to be permanent and immutable.

From the thirteenth through the twentieth centuries the dominant influence was that of Aristotelian-Thomistic philosophy. It is vitally important to keep this emphasis in mind. For it is only in the context of permanent, immutable essences that one can understand the difficulty connected with Pope Paul's encyclical on birth control, *Humanae Vitae.*

Today other philosophical influences have exerted a great effect upon Catholic thinking. We might single out three in particular. The first would be that of existentialist phenomenology which places a great deal of emphasis upon the existence of the individual rather than the individual's essence. The second would be the school of "Process Philosophy" in which much greater emphasis is placed upon man as an individual, growing being, rather than a fixed, permanent, immutable substance. The third new philosophical influence is that of the British schools of linguistic analysis, in which great emphasis is placed upon the meaning of words, words as used in this particular context.

It is not surprising then that we find ourselves bewildered by an ever-increasing and accelerating rate of change. Granted the phenomenal changes in transportation and in communication, granted the fantastic proliferation of printed material, granted the increased influences of totally new and totally different philosophical schools of thought, it is no wonder that we are bewildered and often confused by change in church teaching. In order to cope with such fantastic changes, some find it much easier to return to answers which they learned twenty-five or thirty years ago. Others respond by hoping that someday soon everything will "settle down so we can get back to the way things used to be." Neither of these approaches seems to be satisfactory, since they both seem to deny the fact of change. Both seem to wish that one could, as it were, turn back the hands of the clock. This simply cannot be. Change has occurred, change is occurring, change will continue to occur and at an even more accelerated pace.

HISTORICAL FACTS OF CATHOLIC THEOLOGICAL CHANGE

As a broad historical introduction let us look back to French theology in the late 1930s. In 1937 the French Jesuit theologian Henri de Lubac published a little book entitled simply *Surnaturel*. In this book Father de Lubac asked the relatively abstract question, "Is it possible for man to have a natural desire of the beatific vision?" Given the tragic state of European politics at that time, this book received little attention in the United States. Other French writers at this time included such names as Jean Danielou, Yves Congar, Henri Bouillard. They represented a school which later came to be known as "The New Theology."

With the outbreak of the Second World War in 1939 attention was diverted from the "new theology" to other more pressing social concerns. But at the end of the war theological writing continued apace. In 1950 Pope Pius XII issued his encyclical letter *Humani Generis*. The encyclical condemned many approaches of the "new theology." Even though no one individual author was condemned by name, many theologians were removed from their teaching positions. The early 1950s marked a period of personal and professional recriminations; many people sought to identify individual authors who might have been implicitly condemned by the 1950 encyclical letter.

In 1959 Pope John XXIII announced his intention to convoke an ecumenical council, the Second Ecumenical Council of the Vatican. In the words of Pope John, the purpose of the Second Vatican Council was to bring about an "aggiornamento" of the church. This purpose was primarily pastoral; it was not intended to define new dogmas, but rather to open the windows—to let in fresh air. During the years 1962 through 1965 the Second Vatican

Council met in a series of four plenary sessions, during which many problems facing the church were discussed. The Council produced sixteen major documents.

In discussing the history of Roman Catholic theology, one can assign many different phases or eras. Thus one can speak of the Patristic Era, the Medieval Period, the Reformation Period and so forth. For our purposes, however, we will single out three different phases: (A) pre-Vatican II theology, (B) the theology of Vatican II itself, and (C) post-Vatican II theology.

It is easy to make a mistake in judging that the pronouncements of an ecumenical council put a complete end to theological progress. Theology and doctrine are constantly growing as an organic whole. This is nothing new. The Council of Ephesus in 431 was succeeded by the Council of Chalcedon in 451. In like manner, the Second Vatican Council announced many principles. It is now up to the church—bishops, clergy, theologians, religious, laity—to implement these principles of Vatican II and develop them further.

THE BASIS FOR CHANGE
IN ROMAN CATHOLIC THEOLOGY

Many persons have asked, "How can Roman Catholic theology and church teaching change?" One of the keys in answering this question is found in Vatican II's decree on Ecumenism which reads as follows: "When comparing doctrines, they [Catholic theologians] should remember that in Catholic teaching there exists an order or a 'hierarchy' of truths, since they vary in their relationship to the foundation of the Christian faith."

This order of hierarchy of Catholic truths is largely unknown to most Roman Catholics, even those who have attended Catholic schools for eight, twelve or even sixteen years. Particularly from the time of the Council of Constance (1414–1418), theologians had developed an elaborate system of theological "notes." These notes indicated degrees or rankings of Catholic truths. In time this system of theological notes became very complicated and complex. In recent times there has been an almost complete rejection of these notes. Yet it is extremely important, indeed essential, for the individual to realize that there are degrees of Catholic teaching.

For practical purposes we may distinguish four such degrees of Catholic teaching. The first would be the level of *dogma*. Items of dogmatic status pertain to the core, to the very center, of Catholic teaching. They would include such fundamental areas as the Trinity, the Incarnation, the very heart and center of the Christian faith. The Roman Catholic accepts and believes these dogmas because God has revealed them.

The second level of Catholic teaching is known as "Official Roman Catholic teaching." One finds on this level items which are not properly revealed by God, but which are nevertheless taught officially by the official teaching authority of the Roman Catholic church. Within the framework of Catholic teaching such items of official church teaching are to be held by all Catholics. Nevertheless, at the same time, within the framework of Catholic theology dissent is possible under certain conditions.

The third level of Catholic teaching includes those items which are held by a consensus or a morally unanimous agreement among Catholic theologians. While these are not items of official church teaching nevertheless they are a part of general Roman Catholic teaching. Dissent from these is also possible under certain conditions.

The fourth level of Catholic teaching includes those items among which there is no general consensus among Catholic theologians. Surprisingly, such questions as a "limbo of infants" and the existence of "individual personal guardian angels" fit into this fourth heading. The individual Roman Catholic is perfectly free to accept or to reject these items, about which there is no general consensus.

Awareness of the existence of such degrees of Catholic teaching is absolutely essential for an understanding of change in Catholic teaching. It is indeed regrettable that Catholics who were well trained in Catholic schools are simply unaware of these degrees. When they hear suddenly of a change, they are surprised, since they have been taught, in general, all items of Catholic teaching on the same level. Most are simply unable to distinguish between items which are matters of dogma and matters about which there is no consensus. Every proposition spoken from a pulpit or written in a book will fit into one of these four categories. One has no right to propose .a matter of dogma as though it were a question of speculation. On the other hand, one has no right to present a matter of speculation as though it were a dogma.

CONCLUSION

While change is uncomfortable, there is nevertheless no reason to fear. We realize that there is a central core of Roman Catholic teaching which will remain unchanged. But the entire history of the church has been one of change, of growth, of development. Our greatest enemy here can be fear, fear of the unknown, fear of the uncertain.

Throughout these two volumes, we shall look together at changes which have taken place and changes that perhaps will take place—in a spirit of openness and honesty with each other. In this way we shall all come closer to the God who has made himself known to us and to the church which brings us together not only as an organization but also as a community.

Chapter 1

WHO IS THE CHURCH?

THE URGENCY of the question, "Who is the Church?" is prompted by the traditional adage, *extra ecclesiam nulla salus*. This adage was formulated in patristic times, when church activities were centered in the Mediterranean area. At that time, it was simply presumed (1) that in this constricted geographical area everyone had heard the gospel preached and, (2) that if one remained outside the church it was through one's own rejection of the gospel and a deliberate unwillingness to cooperate with God's grace.

In the year 251, St. Cyprian of Carthage compared the church to Noah's ark. It was all quite simple—either one was on the ark and saved or one was not and was lost. Later, as the church expanded and new lands were discovered, the same line of thinking prevailed. The apex was reached with Pope Boniface VIII (1302), who wrote:

> That there is only one holy catholic and apostolic church we are compelled by faith to believe and hold, and we firmly believe in her and simply confess her, outside whom there is neither salvation nor remission of sins. . . . Furthermore, we declare, state and define that it is absolutely necessary for the salvation of all men that they submit to the Roman Pontiff.

INFLUENCE OF ROBERT BELLARMINE

Around the time of the Council of Trent, one of the chief exponents of the Roman Catholic Counter Reformation was Robert Bellarmine, the Tuscan Jesuit who became a Doctor of the Church. Bellarmine's influence on Roman Catholic theology of the church for the next four centuries was very strong. He stressed very much the *visibility* of the church of Christ, which was, in his own words, "as visible as the Republic of Venice."

For Bellarmine, three conditions were necessary for church membership: (1) reception of the same sacraments, (2) profession of the same faith, and (3) acceptance of the same ecclesiastical authority—namely, that of the Roman Pontiff and the bishops associated with him. Some have summarized Bellarmine's conditions by calling them simply a unity in the church of cult, creed, and code. Thus, church membership became a relatively cut-and-dried, either/or proposition. One either fulfilled these three conditions, in which case one was really a member, or one did not, in which case one was not really a member.

In the sixteenth century, an era of global exploration, Bellarmine's criteria created many problems. What of the countless millions who had never heard the gospel preached? It was at this time that a famous distinction was made between membership in the church in reality (*in re*) and membership in the church by desire (*in voto*). Church membership by desire was further subdivided to include *explicit desire* (e.g., a catechumen taking instructions) as well as *implicit desire* (e.g., the good pagan seeking to do what is right).

In 1854, for the first time in official Roman Catholic teaching, Pope Pius IX introduced the notion of invincible versus vincible "ignorance." Thus, the Pope wrote: "It is to be held as a matter of faith that no one can be saved outside the apostolic Roman church. It is the only ark of salvation and anyone who does not enter it must sink in the flood. But it is equally to be held as certain that those who live in ignorance of the true religion, if such ignorance be invincible, will not be held guilty in the eyes of the Lord."

In 1943 this manner of approach reached its climax in Pope Pius XII's encyclical letter *Mystici Corporis,* wherein the Pope repeated Bellarmine's conditions for *real* membership in Christ's church, stating:

> Only those are to be accounted really members of the church who have been regenerated in the waters of baptism and profess the true faith, and have not cut themselves off from the structure of the Body by their own unhappy act or been severed therefrom, for very grave crimes, by the legitimate authority.

In August of 1949, the Holy Office sent a letter to the Archbishop of Boston, Richard Cushing, concerning the "Boston Heresy Case" (involving Jesuit Leonard Feeney). This letter stressed that a salvific desire to be a member of the church could certainly be implicit, provided, of course, that such a desire be informed and characterized by supernatural faith and supernatural love.

THE TEACHING OF VATICAN II

On November 21, 1964, the Second Vatican Council proclaimed its Dogmatic Constitution on the Church (*Lumen Gentium*). This dogmatic constitution indicated a marked change and progress from earlier Catholic thought, especially in Sections 14–16.

For the most part, Section 14 repeats traditional Roman Catholic teaching regarding the necessity of membership in the church for salvation and remarks: "They are fully incorporated in the society of the church who, having the spirit of Christ, accept her entire system and all the means of salvation given to her, and are united with her as part of her visible bodily structure and through her with Christ who rules her through the Supreme Pontiff and the bishops. The bonds that bind men to the church in a visible way are profession of faith, the sacraments, and ecclesiastical government and communion." However, Section 14 makes two additional points of special interest. First of all, the Council Fathers remind us that individuals are not saved "who though part of the body of the church do not persevere in charity." Secondly, the Council Fathers point out explicitly that catechumens who seek with explicit intention to be incorporated into the church are by that very intention joined with her. "With love and solicitude Mother Church already embraces them as her own."

Section 15 goes even further. In this section the Council Fathers discuss the relationship of the church with other Christians who are not Roman Catholic. The constitution states explicitly, "the church recognizes that in many ways she is linked with those who, being baptized, are honored with the name of Christian, but do not profess the faith in its entirety or do not preserve unity of communion with the successor of Peter."

Section 15 then proceeds to explain this "linking" by citing the following points of contact. First of all, there is common acceptance of the Sacred Scriptures. Then there is a common belief in God and in Christ. There is also a consecration by baptism "in which they are united with Christ." Again there is a common reception of some sacraments. And there is common devotion to Mary, the Mother of God. Furthermore, there is "some true union with the Holy Spirit." Finally, there is, at times, the bond of martyrdom.

Section 16 attempts to deal with non-Christians, stating: "Finally, those who have not yet received the gospel are related in various ways to the people of God." The same Section 16 then continues to discuss several degrees of relationship dealing first of all with Jews, secondly with Moslems, thirdly with non-Christian theists, and finally with atheists.

We note in reference to Sections 14–16 the following three points:

A. There is a deliberate choice of strong words here: (1) Catechumens are "joined with" the church. (2) Other Christians are "linked with" the church. (3) Other non-Christians are "related to" the church. These are indeed strong words coming from an ecumenical council. In previous years even the name "churches" was denied to many Christian assemblies.

B. Reference is made to union with Christ through baptism. This same concept of union with Christ through baptism is repeated in other Council documents. It is difficult to understand how one can be related to Christ through baptism and yet not be somehow a part of Christ's church.

C. In discussing church membership, there is a deliberate avoidance of the term "really" in favor of the term "fully." How does one explain this avoidance? The word fully seems to imply a shift away from an either/or concept of church membership to a concept of membership in varying degrees. That is, one can be a more or less complete member of Christ's church. In times past, one could apply Bellarmine's simple "check-list" and ascertain church membership. In the light of Vatican II's Dogmatic Constitution on the Church, one has a greater or lesser share in church membership according to the degree of one's commitment.

Some authors have attempted to explain this apparently radical change in Catholic teaching by retaining traditional norms of church membership and considering them as external or "sacramental" signs of one's commitment to the church. They would then interpret Vatican II in the light of adding an additional dimension, namely that of internal or dynamic dedication, to the external elements of sacramental or signed membership.

In other words, the sixteenth-century Spanish Jew who, because of social and economic pressures, converted to Roman Catholicism could very easily satisfy Robert Bellarmine's external concepts of church membership. Yet this same person while out-wardly receiving Christian sacraments, professing Christian faith and accepting church authority, could remain at heart a Jew. The question then becomes one of whether he is sincere within himself in professing Christianity. Vatican II seems to address this question very well. Not only must there be an external, sacramental, sign affiliation with the church, but also there must be an internal dynamic commitment to the ideals of Christ in order for one to attain full church membership.

This argument is further supported by reference to *Lumen Gentium's* Section 8, which reads:

> This church constituted and organized in the world as a society, subsists in the Catholic church, which is governed by the successor of Peter and by the bishops in his communion, although many elements of sanctification and of truth may be found outside of its visible structure, which as gifts belonging to the church of Christ, are forces impelling toward Catholic unity.

We note here a striking point of similarity between *Lumen Gentium's* Section 8 and Section 14. Section 8 *deliberately avoided* saying that Christ's church *is* the Roman Catholic church and stated rather that Christ's church *subsists* in the Roman Catholic church. Section 14 states that "they are *fully* incorporated *into the society of the church*" who meet the traditional requirements.

A definite distinction is drawn here between Christ's church as community and Christ's church as organization. Can Christ's church function as community without organization? Can Christ's church function as organization without community? We feel that the answers to these questions are already contained in the documents of Vatican II and in church documents released after the end of this Council.

Chapter 2

WHAT IS CHRIST'S CHURCH?

DURING the past few years, there have been many changes in our way of looking at the church. We have discussed some of these, pertaining to church as community, in the first chapter, "Who is the Church?" Now we turn to changes pertaining to the church as an institution. Three items in particular stand out—the use of different images to describe the church, a different idea of church-state relations, and a different concept of forms of church government.

IMAGES DESCRIBING THE CHURCH

Over the centuries, a great many images have been used to describe the church. Recent changes of imagery have startled many, but there is no cause for alarm.

The New Testament uses approximately ninety-six images to describe Christ's church—such as the salt of the earth, the people of God, Israel, a holy nation, the bride of Christ, the body of Christ, a sheepfold, the heavenly Jerusalem, and so forth. As times changed and people changed, different images acquired very different meanings.

Thus Clement of Alexandria (c. 200) was able to speak allegorically of the church as existing "before the sun, the moon, and the stars." St. Augustine spoke of an "objective redemption" of mankind. For Augustine the very decision that God would become man marked the beginning of the church.

Indeed, for many centuries the main image of the church for most Roman Catholics was that of the "Kingdom of God." Such usage was quite understandable since in Europe the prevalent form of society in those times was feudal and monarchical. But as forms of society changed, the images of the church took on different meanings.

Preliminary documents of the First Vatican Council (1869–70) had proposed a general discussion of the church in its image of "Mystical Body of Christ." However, due to political factors and the outbreak of the Franco-Prussian War, the topic was never formally discussed at that council. Finally, in 1943, Pope Pius XII issued an encyclical letter on the Mystical Body of Christ—*Mystici Corporis*. Times, however, kept changing at an ever accelerating pace, and so also did possible church images.

In its Dogmatic Constitution on the Church, the Second Vatican Council used many scriptural images—sheepfold, flock, field of God, building and temple of God, and spouse of Christ (Chapter 1). Moreover, the Council Fathers proceeded to devote the entire second chapter of that same document to another scriptural image, that of the "People of God."

There is a difficulty in this manner of speaking. As the late Gustave Weigel put it: "You simply cannot make an image into a concept. Just because the church is called the flock of the shepherd does not give any theologian the right to argue that all Catholics are sheep. It is the beauty and the weakness of an image that it cannot be logically worked out by deduction from an *a priori* set of abstract definitions. What is required is an insight into the image used, in terms of the original context in which the image was formed. Then one must try to express this insight in logical propositions that will permit deduction. This is a dangerous enterprise because the individual may, innocently enough, understand the image to say things it was never meant to say" (*America,* December 7, 1963, pp. 730–31).

The special location of this second chapter on the "People of God" has a twofold significance: (1) It reminds us that we are called by God to be saved not only as individuals, but also as members of a community, God's own people. In other words, as we work out our salvation, we don't have to "go it alone." We have brothers and sisters to help, comfort, console, and guide us in our hours of need, just as we are there to help them. (2) It reminds us that the words "hierarchy," "institution," and "church" are not identical. For many years people tended to identify the church with the hierarchy. Even restricting the term "churchman" to the clergy reflected this tendency.

At the Second Vatican Council the Fathers decided to insert this second chapter as a sort of overview of the entire church and as a real introduction to the following chapters on hierarchy, laity, and religious. It thus serves to put these following chapters in their own proper perspectives—that while there are varying ministries of service within the church, we are all equal in our dignity as part of the people of God, that we are indeed "a chosen race, a royal priesthood, a holy nation, a purchased people . . . who in times past were not a people, but are now the people of God" (1 Peter 2:9–10).

The church, then, is not identified with pope, cardinals, bishops, priests, and deacons. At the same time, one must also recall that "People of God" does not *replace* "Mystical Body," "Kingdom of God," or "Bride of Christ." This renovated image simply provides a new insight into the same underlying reality, the church of Christ.

RELATION OF CHURCH AND STATE

In its earliest days, the primitive Christian community was in many ways "an underground church," persecuted in varying degrees by the Roman government. The question of church-state relations was relatively simple—one of church survival.

With the Edict of Constantine in 313, things began to change. Not only was Christianity tolerated, but it became the empire's official religion. It was quite logical, then, that patterns of church government began to resemble those of the imperial government. Thus, just as Rome (the "city of man") had its Caesar governing the state, so also Rome (the "city of God") had its Pope governing the church.

As the political power of the Roman Emperor declined in the west, that of the Roman church increased. By the time of Leo the Great (Pope Leo I, 440–461) the papacy had assumed, in the words of one modern historian, these proportions, "except upon two matters—the pope's independent supremacy over any general council (which was still disputable in the seventeenth century), and his infallibility (which was not *de fide* until 1870)—the dogmatic constitution of 1870 is largely an expansion of St. Leo's doctrine."

Thus, it was not surprising that rivalry occurred between church and state, between emperor and pope. Such rivalry reached its climax between 1073 (when the monk Hildebrand was elected as Pope Gregory VII) through 1198 (election of Pope Innocent III), through 1303 (death of Pope Boniface VIII after the intervention of King Philip the Fair of France).

During these 230 years the *direct* power of the pope over temporal matters was clearly asserted on many occasions. The twentieth-century reader is perhaps awed by the sight of Emperor Henry IV kneeling in the snows of Canossa seeking absolution from Pope Gregory VII and is perhaps equally awed by the sight of Pope Boniface VIII being attacked by mercenaries of King Philip of France.

At the height of this conflict, some Roman Catholic writers asserted that there was in Christendom one "royal power," that of the pope, and that "temporal rulers were instituted, could be judged, and even deposed by the pope."

In the sixteenth century, Robert Bellarmine rejected the notion of any *direct* power of the pope over temporal matters, although in Bellarmine's opinion the pope did maintain an *indirect* power, according to which the pope could depose sovereigns, but only if "it be necessary for the salvation of souls." It seems that the last attempt at papal deposition was that tried by Pope Pius V against Queen Elizabeth I (1570).

We note with interest that prior to the opening of the First Vatican Council (1869–70), many European governments were worried that the council would try to reassert these powers, direct or indirect, of deposition. Such apprehension had some foundation in the syllabus of errors, published by Pope Pius IX on December 8, 1864, which contained a condemnation of the Doctrine of Separation of church and state (Article 55).

During the last 80 years, relatively little was written on this sensitive issue. It was an American Jesuit priest who was able to bring the uniquely American concept of separation of church and state to the attention of the Council Fathers at the Second Vatican Council.

For many years, John Courtney Murray had sought to inform the world that the United States of America had a unique type of government, involving a true separation of church and state—a separation that was based on a pluriformity of religious beliefs. To many continental European minds, such a separation of church and state was incomprehensible.

It was largely through the efforts of Father Murray and of the late Cardinal Albert Meyer of Chicago that the Council's decree on religious liberty was passed. In other words, no longer need the state dominate the church. Likewise, the church need not seek to dominate the state. They are two separate, although related, entities. They must remain separate to perform their proper functions in society as a whole.

FORMS OF CHURCH GOVERNMENT

Just as the Roman imperial government influenced structures of church government, so too, modern forms of democracy also influence church government today. There are two terms here which have been widely used but perhaps little understood. These terms are "collegiality" and "shared responsibility." Let us look at both of these terms more closely.

COLLEGIALITY. This is a technical term applied to the College of Bishops succeeding to the College of the Apostles. Even the most traditional manuals of systematic theology taught such collegiality as a dogma of Catholic faith. Instead of teaching something new, the Second Vatican Council merely re-emphasized this traditional Catholic teaching. A practical emphasis was given by the very meeting of the Second Vatican Council itself. Further practical emphasis was given by Pope Paul VI on September 15, 1965, when he announced his intention to develop a synod of bishops. Since that time the synod of bishops has met regularly with the pope every other year.

SHARED RESPONSIBILITY. This concept is of far more basic and fundamental importance. For it goes to the national and local levels of church policy. The notion of shared responsibility is not totally dependent on the position of Belgian Cardinal Leo Suenens; it is contained throughout the documents of the Second Vatican Council. For example, we may cite the following:

1. A mandate to establish *senates of priests.* Thus it is stated, "in order to put these ideals into effect, a group or senate of priests representing the presbytery should be established (*habeatur*). It is to operate in a manner adapted to modern circumstances and have a form and norms to be determined by law."
2. Moreover, the Second Vatican Council issues a strong recommendation that there be *diocesan pastoral councils.* Thus we read: "It is highly desirable that in each diocese a pastoral council be established over which the diocesan bishop himself will preside and in which specially chosen clergy, religious, and laity will participate. The function of this council will be to investigate and to weigh matters which bear on pastoral activ-

ity, and to formulate practical conclusions regarding them."
3. Moreover, in the documents of the Second Vatican Council there are specific recommendations that *episcopal conferences* in neighboring countries should *cooperate* with each other.
4. Finally, there are specific recommendations that national offices be established, even where local diocesan offices already exist, in such areas as ecumenism, catechetics, and social communications (Decree on the Implementation of *Inter Mirifica,* No. 174, May 23, 1971).

CONCLUSION

We feel that this implementation decree is most significant. Approved specifically by the Holy Father, this decree states explicitly: "Those who exercise authority in the church will take care to insure that there is responsible exchange of freely held and expressed opinion among the people of God. More than this, they will set up norms and conditions for this to take place" (section 116).

Again we read: "The normal flow of life and the smooth functioning of government within the church requires a steady two-way flow of information between ecclesiastical authorities at all levels and the faithful as individuals and as organized groups. This applies to the whole world; to make this possible, various institutions are required. These may include news agencies, official spokesmen, meeting facilities, pastoral councils, all properly financed" (section 120).

Chapter 3

THE DEVELOPMENT OF DOCTRINE

W HEN talking about changes in the Catholic church and in the magisterium, many individuals have the mistaken impression that such church teachings have always remained the same. As we have seen and shall see throughout these two volumes, such is not the case. Change has always been present, but in two different ways—changes in church law or government and changes in church doctrine or teaching. Frequently these two areas have been confused with each other.

One instance of these changes will suffice as an example. Many older Roman Catholics remember when the "eucharistic fast" regulations prevailed. One was not allowed to drink even a little water after midnight before receiving the Eucharist. If one did so, even by accident, one was not allowed to receive Holy Communion later that day. This legislation was changed gradually, in several stages, during and after World War II. Although this was merely a change of *law* and not of teaching, many Roman Catholics felt that a major doctrinal change had occurred.

INTRODUCTORY COMMENTS

In this chapter we wish to discuss changes in Roman Catholic theology and *teaching*. Changes in law are readily understood if the reader recalls the classic adage, "If the church has made a law, the church can always change that law."

But can the church change and develop or even reverse its theological and doctrinal teaching? The answer is a qualified yes. It is qualified in this sense: There are certain central core doctrines ("dogmas") which cannot be changed (e.g., God is Triune, Jesus is God-Man). It is true that clearer formulations may be stated and that deeper insight can be gained into such dogmas through theological reasoning, but the core notions themselves cannot be negated. In fact, Pope John XXIII cited the clearer formulations or expressions of dogma as one of his main intentions in convoking Vatican II.

But when one discusses development of doctrine, one usually understands a deeper question—can there actually be a development, a progression of dogma in such a way that a Christian in the twentieth century would actually believe something which was not believed in the tenth or eleventh centuries? Again the answer is yes. For instance, the Marian doctrines of the Immaculate Conception and the Assumption seem to be contained not even in a formal-implicit way in the New Testament. For many centuries they were either denied or simply not believed as dogmas of divine faith. And yet today they are both defined dogmas.

HISTORICAL BACKGROUND

The Pastoral Epistles seem to speak of a "deposit of faith" which was entrusted to the Apostles and which was to be both preached and safeguarded. Thus we read: "Timothy, take care of all that has been entrusted to you" (1 Tim. 6:20) and also, "Guard the treasure put into our charge, with the help of the Holy Spirit who lives in us" (2 Tim. 1:14). Theologians have referred to Christ's mandate (Mt. 28:20) to teach all nations to "observe all the commands I gave you." Further attention was given to John 21:25, where it is written: "There were many other things that Jesus did; if all were written down in detail, I suppose the whole world would not hold all the books that would have to be written."

In postbiblical times, however, the facts were evident. Change did occur—what did the Trinity and the God-Manhood of Christ mean in terms of Greek philosophy? How could these facts be clearly conveyed to the layman? Serious problems arose, even after the Council of Nicaea (325).

Let us cite several instances. In 376, St. Jerome wrote to Pope Damasus, saying:

> Make a decree, I pray. If it is your pleasure, I shall not fear to say "three *hypostases*" (persons). If it is your bidding, let a new creed be established succeeding the Nicene, and let us be declared orthodox while using the same terms as the Arians. . . . Let nothing be said, if it please you, concerning three *hypostases* and let there be held to be but one. . . . Wherefore I implore Your Beatitude by the Crucified, the Salvation of the World, by the consubstantial Trinity, that I may be authorized by your letters either to refrain from saying *hypostases* or to say it (Letter #15).

Moreover, both Saints Basil and Gregory Nazianzen had grave misgivings about affirming the divinity of the Holy Spirit.

Thus, three of the greatest Fathers of the early church wondered and quibbled about one of the most central doctrines of Christianity, the Trinity. These—along with Nicaea's emphasis on Christ's divinity, Ephesus' emphasis on Christ's substantial unity, and Chalcedon's emphasis on Christ's humanity—provide a striking instance of doctrinal development in the early church.

If we look at this problem from a different viewpoint, we find that the New Testament passages cited above form the basis and the core of the classic Roman Catholic-Protestant debate about the Bible and tradition. (One or two sources of revelation? "Scripture alone?" or "Scripture plus Tradition?")

While a number of fundamentalist groups still hold to a strict "scripture alone" doctrine, most respected Protestant and Roman Catholic scholars have in recent years moved closer together on this issue. Although the debate remains unresolved, Vatican II did facilitate discussion by avoiding the "one or two sources" terminology and by speaking instead in terms of scripture always being understood in relation to the believing community.

PHILOSOPHICAL PRESUPPOSITIONS

To properly understand the question of the development of doctrine, one must realize that there are various philosophical views about the very function and purpose of religious discourse. Pope Pius XII told Bible scholars in his encyclical *Divino Afflante Spiritu* (1943) that they must pay careful attention to the "literary form" in which the various books of the Bible are written—some are written as poetry; others, as letters; others, as historical narratives. Each must be read and interpreted accordingly.

Among linguistic analysts, there are three main views of religious discourse. Some hold that such discourse is essentially *propositional*. That is, religious discourse consists in a set of true-false propositions, which express the entire reality with which they are concerned. Others hold to an essentially *emotive* function of religious discourse. For these, the primary function of religious discourse is found in the emotions which it evokes in the human person hearing it—for example, reassurance, trust, fear. Still others hold to the *ethical* function of religious discourse. For these, religious discourse, no matter what the words themselves may state, is nothing more than a public expression of one's personal commitment to a way of life, an ethic.

It must be admitted that in the past Roman Catholic theology was primarily concerned with the propositional content. However, theologians realize today that to understand religious discourse in its fullness involves a perception and a realization of all three of these functions.

Granted, therefore, a "deposit of faith," it was presumed by many that revelation as such was entirely propositional. In other words, divine revelation in this view consisted in a finite number of propositions made known by God. Indeed, some commentators spoke of the inspired authors of the Bible acting almost as "secretaries" who took dictation from God.

Moreover, granted such a "propositional" view of revelation, it was then presumed that the twelve Apostles possessed exactly the same propositional faith-content which modern man has. A striking instance of this viewpoint is found in 19th-century writing. The most widely read American Roman Catholic editor and author of that period, Orestes A. Brownson, held this opinion very strongly and used it as one of his principal arguments against Cardinal Newman.

Finally, if we consider all of this together—a totally propositional "deposit of faith" and the notion that the twelve Apostles had the same propositional faith-content as ourselves—it is not at all surprising that the traditional Roman Catholic view on the development of dogma proceeded as it did.

In such a context, development of doctrine or of dogma occurred only when there was a process from what was formally-explicitly revealed to that which was formally-implicitly contained therein. But in recent years there has been a major change here. As two examples, let us consider Cardinal John Henry Newman and Father Karl Rahner.

NEWMAN AND RAHNER

Cardinal Newman's famed *Essay on the Development of Doctrine*, although it was written before his conversion to Roman Catholicism, was published shortly afterward (1845). In this volume he described doctrinal development not merely as a simple implicit-explicit transition, but rather as a process of total organic growth.

In his *Essay*, Newman assigned seven general criteria according to which a true doctrinal development must be judged:

1. There must be a conservation of the same *type,* as a result of which the present-day church continues to possess the same qualities as the church of the first centuries.
2. There must be a *continuity* of the same fundamental principles which are applied in every doctrine and in practice.
3. There must be manifested a power of *assimilation.* This means that the church incorporates into herself whatever she finds to be good or true in the world about her.
4. There must be a *logical consistency,* in virtue of which doctrines made explicit at a later era and customs that later came into vogue harmoniously blend in with both the church's principles and with one another.
5. There must have been *some anticipation* of future events. This means that in questions of development there should be found among ancient Christians dim foreshadowings of beginnings of doctrines and practices of later ages.
6. Development should involve a *preservative* addition to antiquity. This seems to mean that new additions do not take away or diminish, but rather corroborate and strengthen matters which were already held much earlier.
7. There must be shown an inexhaustible *vigor* with which the church, in developing her doctrine and worship and organization, neither perishes nor grows old, but instead acquires new strength in proceeding forward.

Although Cardinal Newman moved away from a strict explicit-implicit notion of doctrinal development, we must note that he still spoke of development primarily in terms of *propositions.* On the other hand, Karl Rahner perceives a nonpropositional element in the development of dogma. For Rahner the very elements of dogma itself are also the elements of true dogmatic development. He lists them as follows:

1. The Holy Spirit and Grace. To deny the supernatural and to proceed outside of a faith-context would be, in Rahner's opinion, to reduce God's saving word simply to the self-understanding of a mere creature.

2. The Magisterium. Rahner definitely sees the juridically embodied teaching office of the church as a major factor in dogmatic development.
3. Concept and Word. Rahner here emphasizes the importance of linguistics and of linguistic philosophy in particular—what does *this* word mean in *this* context? (Parenthetically we may note here the linguistic misunderstanding of the terms *"anathema sit"*—let it be condemned—and *"jure divino"*—by divine law or right—as used by the Council of Trent. Many authors of manuals considered these terms to be automatic condemnations of heresy or proclamations of dogma. Today, however, historians realize that these terms had a wide variety of meanings even at Trent itself.)
4. Tradition, understood in a wide sense. Without becoming involved in the classic debate described above, Rahner correctly perceives that even the Reformers could not separate themselves from classical patristic interpretations of the Bible.
5. The acknowledged presence of dogma *as* dogma, as revealed by God. The problem of development, Rahner continues, is that this datum of *consciousness* was not always present. He speaks also of an "intuitional sense" found in the church as a whole.

This fifth point is central to Rahner's notion of development. Walter Burghardt, in discussing this matter, notes that for Rahner:

> In its deepest dimension doctrinal explication is not a movement from proposition to proposition, but a movement from prereflective possession of an entire truth to its more reflective, though necessarily only partial, appropriation in and through propositional formulation (*Theology in Transition,* p. 163).

As is typical with most Karl Rahner statements, the reader is left bewildered and asking, "What does this mean?" Perhaps we can try to unravel it somewhat.

Rahner agrees that there are propositional formulations of the Roman Catholic faith. But he distinguishes between such faith-propositions and those of mathematics and geometry. These latter, he asserts, tend to have a rather fixed and precisely determined content.

However, he continues, dogmatic propositions, while they do have a rather fixed *minimum* content, also have an undetermined *maximum* content. By way of example, Rahner cites the biblical assertion that "Christ died for us." But further questions arise. What is death? What is dying-for-us? In a proposition, Rahner continues, certain ideas are asserted, both explicitly and implicitly. But, over and above this, certain notions are also "communicated." What does death mean for the person who has not yet experienced it? Can one say that such a meaning is conveyed even implicitly in the assertion that "Christ died for us?"

CONCLUSION

We do not wish to omit mention of the work of Bernard Lonergan in this area. He speaks of doctrinal development in terms of a complex historical process which involves three dimensions of motion—the "transcultural," the "theological," and the "strictly dogmatic." However, although Father Lonergan has published several partial studies in this area of development, his promised definitive work has not yet appeared.

Traditional studies admitted that there were various occasions in which a development of doctrine could occur. Historically speaking, they admitted that the most frequent occasion was that of condemning a heresy. Other occasions included advances in philosophical and natural sciences, more mature intellectual reflection, and liturgical practices of the universal church.

However, the facts remain the same. There has been dogmatic development within the Roman Catholic Church—such development continues and will continue. New terms, such as Newman's "illative sense" and Rahner's "preconceptual" knowledge will emerge. The balance between the immutable and the changeable remains as a sign of growth.

Chapter 4

GRACE AND RECONCILIATION

For many years Roman Catholics learned from various catechisms that "grace" is a supernatural gift from God to aid men in the pursuit of their salvation. These same catechisms distinguished two sorts of grace: "sanctifying," which *makes* men children of God, and "actual," which *helps* men to act as children of God, overcoming temptations which might obstruct their progress.

By way of introduction, then, we wish to consider the notion of reconciliation itself and also the historical development of the theme of grace and reconciliation.

THE IDEA OF RECONCILIATION

In most traditional manuals, the notion of reconciliation was indeed included, but it was discussed primarily in the same terms used to describe sin—that of a one-to-one affair between a transcendent God and an individual sinful human being. In this context, little attention was paid to the community aspects of human life. Thus, original sin was discussed mostly in terms of removing the "stain" which separated the individual from God. And sins against the virtue of justice were almost always treated in the context of individual restitution—how much does A have to repay B from whom A has stolen this article?

Not surprisingly, sacramental theology followed suit. If one may speak in general terms, Baptism was seen as a means of

36

removing the stain of original sin; the Holy Eucharist was a sort of reward for being free from the stains of both original and actual sin; the Anointing of the Sick was seen as a "last chance" to be freed from both stains. The reader notes that all of this was regarded primarily in terms of reconciling the individual sinner with an individual God.

This reconciliation was accomplished in an almost mechanical way. Thus, traditional terminology spoke of the sacraments producing grace almost automatically—*ex opere operato*—by virtue of the performance of the external rite. In other words, as long as the recipient did not "place an obstacle," the external sacramental rite produced its effect of either inducing or increasing divine grace.

But recently there has been much talk about the sacraments of Baptism, Penance, Holy Eucharist, and the Anointing of the Sick as involving reconciliation not only with God, but also with the church, or with a particular believing community. Such writers recall Paul's previously cited comments about the incestuous Corinthian man and also raise the question of whether individual sacramental absolution, even in terms of "due compensation" and "removal of scandal," is sufficient. For, they wonder, what harm has this man caused the Corinthian church? What were the social effects of his actions?

To put it briefly, reconciliation is seen today not only as a personal relation between an individual member of the church and God, but also as a social relation between the individual believer and the community of which he or she is a member.

BIBLICAL BACKGROUND

Let us mention a brief word of warning at the very beginning of this section. If there is any one single concept which has acquired countless connotations during the development of Christian theology in both Roman Catholic and Protestant schools, it is that of "grace." The reader must, therefore, be extremely cautious not to read back into the Bible such later theological controversies.

To be quite frank, the Old Testament does very little by way of formulating a theology of grace. True, these books do speak often of God and his people and his many interventions on their behalf, such as in the Exodus narratives. But overall, God's "grace" seems to be considered mainly in the context of divine favor or disfavor toward his people as a whole. Some modern authors, we feel, have tried to read back into Old Testament writings much more than is actually contained there.

The New Testament, however, bespeaks a tension which has perdured throughout all of Christian church history. On the one hand, the extremely complex sixth chapter of John cites Jesus saying, "No one can come to me unless he is drawn by the Father who sent me" (v. 44). Somewhat later, Jesus is quoted as saying that all believers depend upon him: "I am the vine, you are the branches. Whoever remains in me, with me in him, bears fruit in plenty; for cut off from me you can do nothing. Anyone who does not remain in me is like a branch that has been thrown away—he withers" (Jn. 15:5–6). Such passages emphasize the absolute necessity of God's grace. No one can come to Christ unless drawn by the Father. Without Christ one withers.

But, on the other hand, the reader perceives that man must cooperate with God's grace, and that a rejection of such grace is possible. Thus, some of the Jews are castigated for rejecting Jesus: "Jerusalem, Jerusalem, you that kill the prophets and stone those that are sent to you! How often have I longed to gather your children, as a hen gathers her chicks under her wings, you refused! So be it! Your house will be left to you desolate" (Mt. 23: 37–38).

Again, one recalls the rich young man who went away sad when he was advised to sell his possessions and follow Jesus. Such passages emphasize the necessity of man's cooperation with God's grace.

Two polarities appear here: God's grace is necessary, but man is free to reject it. Theologians have grappled with this problem for centuries.

POSTBIBLICAL DEVELOPMENTS

Several centuries after the biblical era, tension developed between two emphases: Which was more important—God's grace or man's cooperation with this grace?

1. *Augustine and the Pelagians.* A monk named Pelagius strongly emphasized the importance of the human element. Saint Augustine strongly emphasized the importance of divine grace, indeed so strongly that he was later accused of an excessive rigorism. In fact, later proponents of extreme forms of predestination cited Augustine as one of their main doctrinal sources.

Shortly thereafter, a modified form of Pelagian teaching appeared which came to be known as "semi-Pelagianism." According to this theory, first steps toward faith, justification, and salvation had to come from man's voluntary free efforts unaided by God's grace. Both Pelagian and semi-Pelagian doctrines were condemned by the Second Council of Orange held in southern France in the year 529.

2. *Later Developments.* The next historical development occurred almost 1,000 years later. In the meantime, however, an obscure Benedictine monk, Gottschalk of Orbais, had briefly revived the question of predestination in the ninth century. At the time of the Protestant Reformation, the related questions of grace, justification, and predestination were raised anew with much vigor. The Reformers hailed Paul, Augustine, and Gottschalk as their champions, while Roman Catholics relied heavily upon Matthew, Augustine, and the Council of Orange as authorities. The debate was climaxed by the Council of Trent (1547) which defined practically the whole of Orange's teaching on justification as Catholic dogma.

After Trent, systematization proceeded rapidly. Using previously mentioned Aristotelian-Thomistic categories, Roman Catholic theologians constructed elaborate theories about grace and justification. Sanctifying grace was considered to be an "accident" added to the soul; the "efficient cause" of this accidental improvement was God himself, while the "instrumental cause" was found primarily in the sacraments.

And so it came to be that many Roman Catholics regarded God's saving grace as a static sort of thing which the just person "accumulated" over a period of time, much after the manner of one's savings account in the local bank. This attitude was typified by frequent discussions about the "reviviscence of merit." If one had X amount of grace, committed a serious sin, and then went to confession, would one still have the same X amount of grace as before the sin? Or would one have to start all over again?

During this same period of systematization, one encounters what is perhaps the most celebrated, or at least the most publicized, Roman Catholic theological controversy of modern times—the Banezian-Molinist controversy *De Auxiliis*. One side, the Banezians, held so strongly to the force of God's grace that they actually held and taught a "physical premotion"—that God would physically move the human person to accept the proffered grace. The other side, the Molinists, held so strongly to human cooperation that they actually taught that God would foresee the response of human wills in such a way that precisely the "proper amount of grace" would be given. While the debate raged hotly, Pope Paul V (1607) forbade either side to label the other as "heretical." But debate still continues even to this day around the same topics—God's omnipotence and man's freedom.

CURRENT TRENDS

This subtle question of grace and reconciliation probably poses more technical theological problems than any other area today. And these technical problems have spilled over into practical life. Why, for example, should there be any church at all? Why confession? It seems that there are several specific problem areas here.

"PERSONALIST" APPROACHES. The systematization of the Roman Catholic theology of grace was mostly dominated by a philosophical approach which was primarily abstract and ontological. However, much greater emphasis is placed today upon so-called personalist approaches, in which man is seen not merely as some sort of abstract "substance" (body and soul) united with many "accidents" (among which one might happen to find grace), but rather as a uniquely individual personal being. While there are different personalist approaches, all writers of this school agree on one point—the primacy of personal values over merely abstract philosophical principles.

It must be admitted that it is difficult to attain a perfect synthesis of these modern approaches with the traditional, defined Roman Catholic teaching. But such a synthesis would have to include philosophers such as Sartre and Marcel, literary authors like Camus, Kafka, and Greene, psychologists like Eric Berne and Eugene Kennedy, as well as such classic theological sources as the councils of Orange and Trent and, of course, biblical and patristic writings. It is this writer's view that the best attempt at such a Roman Catholic synthesis is found in Charles Meyer's *A Contemporary Theology of Grace.*

RECONCILIATION WITH THE CHURCH. This expression has attracted much attention recently, especially with regard to certain sacraments. Proponents of this approach allow that the social aspects of sin have always been admitted, but have never been sufficiently emphasized by Roman Catholic theologians. Moreover, these same proponents contend, serious sin offends *both* God *and* the believing community.

They consider sacraments in a manner somewhat different from that taught in the Baltimore Catechisms, all of which spoke in terms of sacraments of the "living" and of the "dead" (Baptism and Penance, respectively). Theologians advocating a more communal view of the sacraments also see the Holy Eucharist and the Anointing of the Sick as sacraments of reconciliation. Their main thrust is that these sacraments involve not only a personal reconciliation with God, but also a communal reconciliation with the church (and thereby with God). And here is where the main problem lies: Which comes first—reconciliation with God or with the church?

There is some ambiguity of terminology here. Most advocates of "reconciliation with the church" admit correctly that "not every serious sinner is legally excommunicated." But, at the same time, many of the same authors contend that reconciliation with the church *precedes* grace and that such reconciliation is the proper cause of grace.

However, theologians opposing this view cite the following words of Trent regarding the sacrament of Penance:

> That which is signified and produced by this sacrament is, so far as its force and efficacy are concerned, reconciliation with God, which sometimes in persons who are pious and who receive this sacrament with devotion is wont to be followed by peace and serenity of conscience (Session 14, Ch. 3).

These words of Trent do admittedly emphasize reconciliation with God, but they do not exclude the necessity of reconciliation with the church.

When talking in the context of "reconciliation with the church," another problem arises in considering venial sins and so-called confessions of devotion. It is quite clear from church practice that the individual may approach the sacrament of Penance with sins which are merely venial or sins which have been previously confessed. Since such offenses do not exclude one from sharing the Eucharist, it is not quite clear how "reconciliation with the church" is involved here. In fact, this is one of the major objections against the various "reconciliation with the church" theories.

LITURGICAL CHANGES. Regardless of one's theological stance concerning reconciliation with the church and its causal relation to God's grace, there has been much greater emphasis upon church as community and the communal aspects of Christian life. Most liturgical changes of the past decade should be viewed from this perspective.

This is especially true regarding the sacraments. Thus, Baptism is seen not just as a rite cleansing a person from all sorts of devils which had previously inhabited him or her, but as a positive ritual of acceptance into the Christian community. Communal exercises of the sacrament of Penance are seen in the same way. While retaining the sacred privacy of the confessional and the strict obligation of confessional secrecy, proponents of this practice feel that there are certain circumstances when an individual may feel better after "talking out" some particular problem with the community.

Likewise, the Holy Eucharist is more frequently regarded as a sacrament of reconciliation. Attempts, sometimes clumsy, have been made to express this—such as a handshake instead of the traditional "kiss of peace." In large urban parishes, some have regarded the notion of shaking hands with a total stranger as ludicrous. But such reforms should be viewed in the words of Christ: "If you are bringing your offering to the altar and there remember that your brother has something against you, leave your offering there before the altar, go and be reconciled with your brother first, and then come back and present your offering" (Mt. 5:23–24). Much the same is said about the Anointing of the Sick, in which serious illness or approaching death is seen not just as an isolated, lonely affair, but one in which the individual receives divine grace, in addition to the support of one's fellow Christians, one's community.

CONCLUSION

At this date, it is impossible to appraise future developments in Roman Catholic theology of grace. Certain constants will remain, as they have for centuries—God's omnipotence and the need for man's cooperation. But the main thrust will be, in our opinion, the reconciliation of these polarities in terms of Christian personalism.

Chapter 5

INFALLIBILITY

DURING the past several years, the "infallibility" both of the pope and of the church as a whole has been discussed frequently and with some vehemence. On July 18, 1870, the First Vatican Council defined as a dogma of divine and Catholic faith the infallibility of the Roman pontiff. Has Roman Catholic teaching on this point changed?

Properly, one should first state traditional Roman Catholic teaching on this matter. To begin with, let us look at infallibility negatively. Infallibility has never been considered to be omniscience. Popes do not know everything about religious matters. Nor does infallibility mean impeccability: Popes can sin.

Rather, by papal infallibility Catholic theologians have traditionally understood that *under certain conditions* the pope will be *preserved* from error. There are three such conditions: (1) The pope must be acting precisely as pope, using the full authority of his papal office; (2) the pope must be teaching something *for the entire church*, not just for a small group or even for a whole country; (3) the pope must be teaching something about *faith or morals*, not about history, politics or anything else. These were the three conditions set down by the First Vatican Council for an *ex cathedra* pronouncement.

45

HISTORICAL BACKGROUND FOR INFALLIBILITY

The New Testament background for the dogma of papal infallibility is rather mixed. Christ had indeed made promises to Peter and to the entire community. Without doubt Peter played a special role in the early Christian community. Moreover, there were specific mandates in the Pauline epistles to preserve and to hold true to teachings which had been handed down. Thus one reads: "Let me warn you that if anyone preaches a version of the gospel different from the one we have already preached to you, whether it be ourselves or an angel from heaven, he is to be condemned" (Galatians 1:8). And again, especially: "Keep as your pattern the sound teaching you have heard from me, in the faith and love that are in Christ Jesus. You have been trusted to look after something precious; guard it with the help of the Holy Spirit who lives in us" (2 Timothy 1:13–14).

But as the tiny Christian community continued to grow and came into contact with Greek philosophy and Roman law, questions arose. What precisely was this gospel teaching, this "deposit of faith," as it came to be called?

In our introduction we spoke of "degrees" of Roman Catholic teaching or of "theological notes." Such distinctions between "levels" or "degrees" of church teaching are almost as old as the church herself.

Thus Prosper of Aquitaine (ca. 430), a disciple of St. Augustine, distinguished between erroneous beliefs which he described as "not Catholic," others as "wrong," others as "deserving severe reproof," and finally, others as "speaking more harshly than we would speak." In other words, Prosper distinguished between errors that were not heretical, that is, between items which pertained to Catholic faith or dogma and items which did not pertain to dogma.

At about the same time, Vincent of Lerins (ca. 434), trying to set some definite rule of faith, established three conditions. Thus, an item of divine faith which must be believed was one which had been always, everywhere, and by all Christians received as a matter of divine faith.

During the twelfth and thirteenth centuries, medieval theologians debated the teaching authority of both the pope and the church. Some (such as Hervaeus of Bourg-Dieu and Stephen Langton) held that the pope could define a new doctrine because of a special revelation which he had received from God. Others (such as the disciples of Peter of Capua) held that the pope's authority in such matters was insufficient unless it was supported by the consent of an ecumenical council. Such discussions continued until well after the Council of Constance.

In official church documents, the Council of Constance (1414–1418) used eight different terms to describe deviations from Roman Catholic teaching. Such errors were described as being either "heretical," "not Catholic," "erroneous," "scandalous," "blasphemous," "offensive to pious ears," "temerarious," or "seditious." A century later, Pope Leo X used similar terms in condemning the teachings of Martin Luther, describing them as "errors," "heretical," "scandalous," "false," "offensive to pious ears," "seductive to simple minds," and "deviating from Catholic truth." In each of these instances church documents, while condemning certain teachings as errors, distinguished between items which went against the core of Catholic teaching and items which did not pertain to this core.

No Roman Catholic really questioned the right and the duty of the church to preserve the "deposit of faith." But at the same time no one really worked out the precise nature of the church's teaching authority in relation to matters which were not dogmatic, pertaining to the core of the gospel message. In fact it was not until 1863, three hundred years after the Council of Trent, that official mention was first made of the church's non-infallible teaching authority. In that year Pope Pius IX wrote a letter to the Archbishop of Munich, pointing out that Catholic theologians were obliged to accept official papal teaching, even when this was not proposed as a dogma. It is only with this background that we can fully understand the teachings of the First Vatican Council regarding papal infallibility.

VATICAN I AND INFALLIBILITY

On December 6, 1864, Pope Pius IX informally announced his intention of convoking an ecumenical council. Public announcement of this ecumenical council was made on June 29, 1867. One year later, on June 29, 1868, a formal bull was issued proclaiming the council, setting December 8, 1869 as the date of the council's opening. During these several years, as in all councils, commissions were formed to draw up preliminary drafts or "working papers" as a basis for conciliar discussion. Five such commissions were established—on faith and dogma, on ecclesiastical discipline and canon law, on religious orders, on oriental churches and foreign missions, and on political, ecclesiastical affairs and relations of church and state.

The original document on the church was distributed to the Council Fathers on January 21, 1870. This document included 15 chapters, beginning with a discussion of the church as the Mystical Body of Christ and ranging through such topics as the primacy of the Roman Pontiff, the infallibility of the entire church, and the relationship between church and state. Chapter 8 of this original working paper dealt with the *indefectibility* of the *church as a whole*, while chapter 9 dealt with the *infallibility* of the *church as a whole* and chapter 11 dealt with the primacy of the Roman Pontiff.

Due to previously mentioned political factors, the questions of papal primacy and of papal infallibility were considered separately and were, indeed, taken out of their original context as a statement on the church as a whole.

Rumors of war between Prussia and France had been prevalent for a long time and had forced acceleration of discussion on the infallibility decree. Facts later bore this out. One day after the final infallibility vote, war was declared between France and Prussia.

Unsuccessful attempts were made to continue the council. But French troops protecting Rome were withdrawn at the beginning of August. Italian troops occupied Rome in the middle of September and Pius IX suspended the council "indefinitely" on October 20, 1870. Now let us look back.

There had been much heated debate about both papal primacy and papal infallibility. On July 13, 1870, a trial vote was taken concerning papal infallibility. The results were as follows: Six hundred and one votes were cast. Four hundred and fifty-one voted affirmatively and without condition. Eighty-eight voted negatively. Sixty-two others voted affirmatively, but only on the condition that certain changes be made in the proposed text.

On July 18, 1870, the final formal vote was taken on papal infallibility. The results of this vote were as follows: 533 affirmative and 2 negative. The 2 negative votes were cast by Bishop Riccio of Cajazzo and by Bishop Fitzgerald of Little Rock, Arkansas. While much attention has been given to Bishop Fitzgerald's negative vote, by far the strongest American opposition to papal infallibility came from Archbishop Peter Richard Kenrick of St. Louis, Missouri. In the opinion of many church historians, Archbishop Kenrick's 100-page objection to papal infallibility remains to this day the strongest attack against this doctrine.

The final text approved at Vatican I reads as follows: "We teach and define that it is a dogma divinely revealed: that the Roman Pontiff when he speaks *ex cathedra,* that is when in discharge of the office of pastor and teacher of all Christians, by virtue of his supreme apostolic authority he defines a doctrine regarding faith or morals to be held by the universal church, by the divine assistance promised him in blessed Peter, is possessed of that infallibility with which the divine redeemer willed that his church should be endowed for defined doctrine regarding faith or morals: and that therefore such definitions of the Roman Pontiff are irreformable of themselves, and not from consent of the church."

BISHOP GASSER'S RELATION

Due to the great heat of conciliar discussion regarding papal infallibility, it was decided that an authoritative explanation of the proposed decree be given by a member of the commission preparing the document. The man selected was Vincent Gasser, Prince-Bishop of Brixen in the Austrian Tyrol. On July 11, 1870, he presented to the Council Fathers his *Relatio* (or explanation) in a speech which lasted almost four hours.

May I pause here for a moment? According to norms validated by Pope Pius XII in his encyclical *Divino Afflante Spiritu* (1943), scholars must examine the Bible in a thorough and methodical manner. They must search out the meaning of words in the original text and try to determine the mind and the intention of the author. In like manner, we must examine official documents of councils and of popes. Why did they choose one word rather than another? What was their intention?

This is the importance of Bishop Gasser's explanation. While not an official conciliar document, it does give us an insight into what the Council Fathers had in mind when defining papal infallibility. Let us single out two main points of Bishop Gasser's explanation:

1. *The relationship of the pope to other bishops.* Gasser remarks: "[The pope] is infallible only when, as teacher of all Christians, that is, as representing the universal church, he judges and defines what is to be believed or rejected. He can no more be separated from the church than the foundation can be separated from the building it bears. Further, we do not separate the pope's infallibility defining from the cooperation and concourse of

the church, at any rate in this sense, that we do not exclude such cooperation and such concourse of the church." And again, ". . . The pope is bound by his office and the gravity of the matter to take means apt for ascertaining the truth and announcing it; in such means are councils, or the council of bishops, cardinals, theologians, etc. These means will be different in different cases and we ought piously to believe that in the divine assistance given to Peter and his successors by Christ there is included a promise as to the means necessary and apt for making an infallible judgment by the pope."

2. *Object of infallibility.* It had been debated whether the pope's infallibility extends only to dogma or to other degrees of church teaching. Gasser restricts infallibility to matters of dogma, stating: "But as it seems right to the fathers of the deputation with unanimous agreement, that this question be not defined now, but be left in the state in which it is, it follows necessarily, that the decree of faith concerning papal infallibility should be so worded as to define, concerning the object of infallibility in the definitions of the Roman Pontiff, that exactly the same is to be believed as is believed concerning the object of infallibility in the definitions of the church."

And again: "But in those things in which it is theologically certain, though not yet certain by faith, that the church is infallible, by this decree of the council the pope's infallibility similarly is not defined to be believed as of faith." In other words, Bishop Gasser's quasi-official explanation makes it quite clear that the pope is ordinarily presumed to consult the universal church and also that papal definitions are restricted to matters of dogma.

Over the past 100 years, since papal infallibility was defined, only one dogma has been infallibly pronounced by a pope. That dogma was the dogma of the Assumption of the Blessed Virgin Mary defined by Pope Pius XII on November 1, 1950.

HANS KUNG'S OBJECTION

In July of 1970, noted Swiss theologian Hans Küng published a book which seemed to deny papal infallibility. This book, entitled *Infallible? An Inquiry* was originally published in both German and Italian and appeared on the American market in April of 1971. In it Küng raises basic questions concerning infallibility. Moreover, the questions which he raises are more philosophical than theological. Thus, he asks whether any proposition can fully and totally explain the truth in a completely unequivocal sense. He admits the necessity of a propositional explanation of faith and he also admits the necessity of dogma and creeds as expressions of this faith. Furthermore, these creeds are of their very nature binding.

But Küng raises an even deeper question. The very item which had been scheduled for discussion at the First Vatican Council concerning the infallibility of the entire church was not discussed at that council. So, Küng asks, if the pope is said to have the same infallibility as that promised to the universal church, and if at the same time the infallibility of the universal church is not all that clear, how can one say that the pope is infallible with regard to defining certain propositions?

In other words, Küng questions, if it is not certain (dogma) that the church as a whole is infallible in the sense of teaching propositions which are antecedently and *a priori* guaranteed to be immune from error, how can one apply these norms to papal pronouncements? The German bishops in their February, 1971, statement wisely observed that, while Küng's book does not uphold certain items of traditional Catholic teaching, nevertheless it does raise questions which should be discussed openly and freely within the church.

The debate continues. It is still premature to state that there has been a major shift in Catholic teaching regarding papal infallibility. Only time will provide answers to these questions.

Chapter 6

SEXUAL MORALITY

U NTIL the recent past, Roman Catholic moral theologians had discussed sexual ethics in extremely guarded, almost secretive, ways. In fact, one highly respected manual of moral theology, written in English by an English author, published its entire section on sexual morality in Latin. It is small wonder, therefore, that for many years Roman Catholics were at best ill-informed concerning technical theological discussions about sexual problems.

When such discussions became more public, and especially at the time of the *Humanae Vitae* controversy (in 1968), many Roman Catholics were shocked and dismayed. Had there been major changes here? We propose to examine this question by looking at biblical teachings, official church teachings, theological reason, and current problems.

HISTORICAL BACKGROUND

Our treatment of this topic is much more historically oriented, since we feel that many Roman Catholics are just not aware of the historical development of church teaching in this area. Consequently, many feel that such teachings have a greater doctrinal value than is warranted. The very first area to which one must turn is the Bible, both the Old and the New Testaments.

OLD TESTAMENT. Sexual teaching here is at best unclear. There is a general prohibition against adultery in the Decalogue in both the priestly (Ex. 20:14) and the deuteronomic versions (Dt. 5:18). The reader also recalls the frequently misinterpreted "Onan incident" (Gn. 38:8–11), as well as the equally often misinterpreted accounts of the destruction of Sodom and Gomorrah (Gn. 18 & 19).

But the account of Lot's daughters having sexual intercourse with their drunken father (Gn. 19:31–38), in addition to the Israelites' polygamous kings, is not easily discussed at mixed parties. True, Lv. 15:16–18 speaks of seminal discharges and Dt. 23:9–11 of nocturnal emissions, but these seem to be in terms of washing one's body for hygienic and ritual purification.

In general, Old Testament writings seem to provide no specific binding rule about premarital coitus. Admittedly, there are condemnations of specific actions: (1) Dt. 23:17–19 and Si. 9:6 seem to condemn prostitution. (2) Dt. 22:13–29 seems to condemn the following acts—(a) a woman deceiving her husband before marriage into thinking that she is a virgin when she is not; (b) rape; (c) a man sleeping with a woman already betrothed to another man. In conclusion then, the Old Testament message is unclear. Given the centuries required for its composition, the reader should not be surprised by this.

NEW TESTAMENT. These writings seem to convey a clearer message. Thus, Paul advises the Corinthian community that the incestuous man should be, to use a later term, "excommunicated" (1 Cor. 5:1–13). There are generic condemnations such as those found in 1 Cor. 6:9–10 stating that certain people who do wrong will not inherit the kingdom of God—"people of immoral lives, idolators, adulterers, catamites, sodomites, thieves, usurers, drunkards, slanderers and swindlers will never inherit the kingdom of God." Similarly, Gal. 5:19–21 states:

> When self-indulgence is at work the results are obvious: fornication, gross indecency and sexual irresponsibility;

idolatry and sorcery; feuds and wrangling, jealousy, bad temper and quarrels; disagreements, factions, envy; drunkenness, orgies and similar things. I warn you now, as I warned you before: those who behave like this will not inherit the kingdom of God.

Moreover, there is the strict warning of Ep. 5:3–5 that there must not even be any mention of fornication or impurity with the caution that "nobody who actually indulges in fornication or impurity or promiscuity—which is worshiping a false god—can inherit anything of the kingdom of God."

What at first glance seems quite clear, however, is not quite that clear at a second reading. Throughout all these passages one encounters the Greek word *porneia*. What did this word mean when the New Testament was being composed? This has, indeed, been one of the most frequently played New Testament "word games," and the final decision concerning the meaning of *porneia* still remains in doubt. It seems that this word, depending upon the context in which it was used, had many different meanings— adultery, incest, prostitution, or sexual promiscuity.

Moralist John F. Dedek attempts, and we think well, to summarize this rather confusing mass of data when he asserts:

"A fair conclusion from a study of the Old and New Testaments is this: While the Bible condemns adultery, incest, prostitution and sexual licentiousness or promiscuity, it is not at all clear that it ever condemns all premarital coitus as sinful, much less premarital petting and sex play" (*Contemporary Sexual Morality,* p. 31).

POSTBIBLICAL DEVELOPMENTS

In tracing these developments, we look to patristic thought, magisterial teaching, and theological reasoning processes.

PATRISTIC THOUGHT. Neo-Platonic, Gnostic, Manichaean, and Stoic influences on the formulation of Christian sexual ethics were rather strong. Quite frequently, the soul was seen in relation to the body as a prisoner in a cell or a rider on a horse. Consequently, it is not surprising that all "bodily" and "sensual" pleasures came to be regarded with some suspicion. Moreover, when these suspicions were correlated with such Old Testament teachings as those regarding the need for purification after a nocturnal emission, the results were quite predictable. Great fathers of the church such as St. Augustine taught that even married couples should refrain from receiving the Holy Eucharist after having sexual intercourse.

Thus, in patristic and later times, the thought continued that all sexual acts, even by married couples, were at best something less than perfect. Later with the revival of Aristotelian philosophy in Thomism, such tendencies became even more pronounced. For under the doctrine of potency and act, all being was conveniently divided and subdivided in terms of matter and form, essence and existence, substance and accident.

In these terms one could analyze sex coolly and antiseptically. One could refer to the Bible and then "reason theologically"—that is, take biblical data and then work out all their ramifications and implications in the framework of a single philosophical system. This is precisely what happened.

THEOLOGICAL REASONING. If the Bible clearly stated that adultery, fornication, incest, homosexual acts, and masturbation were wrong and, moreover, that one was excluded from the kingdom of God by committing some transgressions, and that one was liable to be destroyed by a rain of fire and sulphur for others, and, finally that a man committed adultery in his heart merely by looking at a woman lustfully (Mt. 5:28), then one could reason as follows within the framework of Aristotelian-Thomistic thought.

First of all, an elaborate and well-reasoned system was developed: There were actions in which sexual pleasure was directly intended. If these were acts between a validly married couple preparatory to intercourse, they were permitted. However, if these acts were not preparatory to intercourse, then the persons involved had to avoid any direct intention of sexual climax. If one were speaking outside of the context of validly married persons, all directly intended sexual gratification was forbidden under pain of mortal sin.

Secondly, if sexual pleasure were not directly intended (in the context of "singles," "unmarrieds," and "marrieds"), then one had to apply the rules regarding "occasions of sin." Such occasions were either "proximate" or "remote" and the individual had to develop a sort of sliding scale of proportionate "excusing causes" to determine the morality of such actions as reading books, dating, holding hands, and kissing. It was all very logical—in the Aristotelian-Thomistic framework. But at the same time, it was also very complicated.

MAGISTERIAL PRONOUNCEMENTS. In considering the plethora of such statements, one must admit that there is a truly extensive range of authentic magisterial pronouncements. We wish to cite several random instances. Thus, one observes Pope Leo IX writing to Peter Damian (1054) that masturbators should not be admitted to major orders. Pope Innocent IV and the Council of Lyons (1245) asserted that "there is no doubt" that fornication, "which an unmarried person commits with another unmarried person," is a serious sin. Pope Pius II condemned (1459) as "most pernicious" the opinion that debauchery outside of marriage was sinful not in itself, but only because it was forbidden by church law.

In 1666, Pope Alexander VII condemned as "at least scandalous" an opinion which regarded masturbation, sodomy, and bestiality as sins of specifically equal malice. And in 1679 Pope Innocent XI condemned, again as "at least scandalous," the opinion that masturbation is not forbidden by natural law. The list reads on, well into the twentieth century. But the reader will note that none of these official pronouncements is presented as a dogmatic definition of faith or morals.

PRACTICAL MORAL PROBLEMS

No one will deny that there are many such problems today, especially regarding sexual morality. We do not pretend to have the answers, but we do wish to offer two practical considerations of special interest to readers in the U.S.A.

The first practical point noted here concerns the influence of "Jansenism." This was a theological and philosophical movement which was especially influential during the 17th and 18th centuries both in France and in the Netherlands. Frequently referring, at times almost naively, to the writings of St. Augustine, the Jansenists seemed to hold in a rather negative way that man was both completely incapable of personal decisions for good and totally at the mercy of what they described as "triumphant concupiscence." The reader recalls that this view was in a way very similar to earlier patristic notions of the soul as a prisoner in a cell.

In moral theology, their position was predictable. They held a position of absolute rigorism—that is, one which proposed extremely rigorous demands with no room for compromise and which insisted that one had to be certain about the lawfulness of an act before doing it. Perhaps unwittingly, many of today's criticisms of excessive "legalism" and "juridicism" in moral theology are still reactions against this extreme Jansenist position which, in the area of sexual morality, was quite consistent with Jansenism's general positions.

Although Jansenism as such was finally and officially condemned by Pope Clement XI in his bull *Unigenitus* (1713), its effects have lingered on. For American readers, these lingering effects have perhaps been most often perceived in the moral teachings of the early French and Irish missionaries, many of whom had been trained in French seminaries, where some sort of Jansenistic backlash was still very strong.

The second major practical pastoral problem has been found

in a frequently oversimplified pastoral presentation of sexual ethics. Recall for a moment the rather complex theoretical structure which we described above regarding direct and indirect intentions, proximate and remote occasions of sin, and also proportionate excusing causes. These are difficult distinctions, even for the professional theological student to master. Let us also recall that the most critical time for prudent education in sexual ethics probably lies in the 13–18 age range (if not earlier, as some say). Furthermore, it is well to remember that young persons at this age are generally not that adept at philosophical niceties and fine points of distinction.

Anyone with practical teaching experience knows the dilemma posed here. On the one hand, the teacher sits down and at great length counsels every person with a question or a problem. But this process is tiring, demanding, and takes much time. On the other hand, the teacher is easily tempted to give quick, oversimplified answers to complex theological and personal problems.

In our own experience, we have personally heard some teachers and missionaries respond to questions in the following manner: "Is kissing always a mortal sin?" "Yes. Next question." "Is going steady a mortal sin?" "Yes. Next question." If one goes "by the book"—in these cases, traditional moral theology manuals —the answers given by these teachers and missionaries are patently false and these respondents simply should have been flunked in Moral Theology or, at least, never have been permitted by a bishop to hear confessions. Today, such men are not considered conservative, but simply ignorant.

AN OVERVIEW

It seems that Roman Catholicism has primarily considered the *functional* aspect of sexual ethics, with morality determined chiefly, if not entirely, in terms of conception or nonconception. This view has recently come under attack for two reasons: (1)

previous consideration of marriage was basically biological (it was only recently that "the marriage act" was even considered as a "remedy for concupiscence"); (2) in a peculiar manner, many of the moralists placed a mistaken emphasis on the male sperm, depending on Greek biological theories and opining that every willful ejaculation of male sperm not leading to conception must be regarded as a moral offense similar to murder.

There has, indeed, been a significant change in Roman Catholic attitudes about sexual morality. Perhaps it cannot be spelled out in precise formulas at present. But the major shift has been toward a more positive view of sex in which sexual activity is seen not as a begrudgingly granted "remedy for concupiscence," but as a positively oriented, human, interpersonal relation.

I will be the first to admit that I take an extremely conservative approach to questions such as this. The first recourse of the Roman Catholic theologian must always be to the Bible. As we have seen, the Bible contains very unclear teachings on such questions. In both Old and New Testament writings most matters are surely not matters of "divine faith from clear Scripture."

The Roman Catholic theologian also turns to what he considers the "divinely appointed magisterium of the church." Again he finds a great mass of "official, but authentic and noninfallible" teaching. However, the theologian can neither dismiss biblical data nor ignore authentic magisterial teaching. Nor can the Roman Catholic present them as matters of divine faith when their dogmatic stature is unclear. This is the heart of the problem.

Chapter 7

THE CHURCH AND SOCIAL ISSUES

DURING the past few years, many persons have observed Roman Catholic priests, nuns and brothers participating in—and sometimes leading—demonstrations in favor of civil rights and antipollution efforts, or against alleged political corruption and the Indochinese War. The response of some has been positive gratitude that churchmen and churchwomen have taken a public stand. The reaction of others has been negative, revulsion against what they consider to be church meddling in politics. Whatever one's response may be, there has been an evident change in attitude here, one which should be investigated.

Part of this change may be attributed to changes in our notions of spirituality. In the past, spirituality had been frequently viewed as a one-to-one relationship between the individual and God. Today there is greater emphasis upon the person not only as an individual, but also as a member of a community. Negatively, this is seen as a reaction against the Marxist dictum that religion is the opiate of the masses, the notion that the oppressed should "offer up" their sufferings to gain a heavenly reward. Positively, it is seen as the realization of the notion that man himself is not merely a "rational" animal, but indeed a "social" one with obligations not only to his immediate neighbors but to all of mankind.

HISTORICAL BACKGROUND

NEW TESTAMENT MATERIAL. We are aware of certain biblical teachings about slavery and we will discuss Catholic teaching about war and peace in the next chapter. Although some of these remarks may sound strange to the modern reader, one is well-advised to recall that the biblical authors and editors were always intent on speaking to men of their own time. Today's reader must always bear this in mind.

Much of previous Roman Catholic discussion about the church and social issues centered about the "coin of tribute" gospel passages (Mt. 22:15–22; Mk. 12:13–17; Lk. 20:20–26). When Jesus had examined the denarius, he replied: "Give back to Caesar what belongs to Caesar—and to God what belongs to God." Many interpreted this passage as meaning either that Jesus had cleverly avoided a trap or that the church should have nothing to do with political matters. Yet as Charles Homer Giblin notes, many of the traditional interpretations have been "overly facile." Giblin comments: "Jesus' answer is not a pat refutation or a skillful evasion of a political difficulty, nor is it presented as a theology of the State; it is a challenge to penetrating understanding of a genuinely theological cast, a challenge that looks to man's discerning his relationship to God in moral conduct" (*Catholic Biblical Quarterly,* Oct. 1971, pp. 510–527).

POSTBIBLICAL BACKGROUND. While some have felt that the church should not become involved in political matters, historical facts seem to go counter to such an opinion. Indeed, the church has been "politically" involved ever since Constantine's decree in 313. As we have seen, interest prior to that time was centered mostly in either survival or martyrdom. But as Catholicism was at first accepted and later received as the Empire's official religion, one sees a gradual development.

At first, the church was considered to be outside of political maneuverings. But then remarkable things happened as emperors began to convoke ecumenical councils. Constantine I convoked Nicaea; Theodosius I convoked Constantinople I; Theodosius II convoked Ephesus; Marcian convoked Chalcedon; Justinian I convoked Constantinople II. The list reads on.

Mutual church-state political involvement increased. The church gradually came to be considered as a bulwark of the political establishment, and vice versa. "The law of the state is next to the law of God" became the cry of stalwarts during this era. Much of the theorizing about this question dates back to the early 9th-century Carolingian period, when the emperor was considered the civil equal of the pope. As we have seen earlier, papal dominance increased strikingly in the early Middle Ages. In the high Middle Ages, the pope was considered to be superior to the emperor; but with the untimely death of Boniface VIII, such speculations came to a practical end. However, the continued development of the "Papal States" kept this political problem alive for six more centuries.

Meanwhile political involvement increased even further. We have already mentioned papal deposition of an emperor. There are portraits of archbishops acting as viceroys of Mexico. In addition to Cardinal Richelieu, we see Talleyrand hailed even today as "Statesman-Priest: The Agent-General of the Clergy and the Church of France at the end of the Old Regime." To this very day we observe papal legations and nunciatures representing the Vatican in many countries, and since the end of the 11th century, we have observed at least 150 papal concordats (or treaties) between the church and various states. Truly, the church has been involved directly in politics. Some readers have, therefore, found the furor about recently elected Jesuit Congressman Robert Drinan a bit strange.

Of course, there has also been an indirect apolitical concern about social issues. Observe the formation of religious orders dedicated to the ransoming of captives, and to the care of the sick, the aged, and orphans. One is also impressed by Cardinal Manning's support of the Liverpool dock workers in their 1891 strike. Manning had supported very strongly the definition of papal infallibility in 1870; given Leo XIII's encyclical on social justice, he backed the workers totally.

THE "MANUAL" APPROACH. The traditional manuals customarily spoke of "justice" in terms of rendering unto others that which is due to them. Those authors, it is true, usually divided their treatment of justice into two areas—*commutative* justice, which dealt with relations between individuals or with institutions organized as legal persons; and *distributive* justice, which dealt with individuals in relation to society as a whole.

In the former, one found discussions of such questions as individual restitution. ("If you stole $5.00 from him, you owe him $5.00 in return.") In the latter, one found such questions as payment of just wages and overpricing. But this area was frequently left extremely vague. ("What of under-the-counter kickbacks and the effect of these upon the entire economy?" Frequently the answer was given: "It is wrong. But for restitution, wait for a legal settlement.") In this manual approach, broader social questions were frequently left unanswered.

RECENT DEVELOPMENTS

Although much of this matter concerning social issues represents official, though noninfallible, church teaching, it would seem that a good portion of it has not been promulgated.

On May 15, 1891, Pope Leo XIII published his memorable encyclical on social justice, *Rerum Novarum*, in which he asserted the right of workers to a living wage and also their right to organize among themselves. Forty years later, Pope Pius XI issued a commemorative encyclical letter, *Quadragesimo Anno*, reasserting and developing further the principles stated by his predecessor. In more recent years, we have had further official yet admittedly noninfallible statements from Pope John XXIII in his encyclicals *Mater et Magistra* and *Pacem in Terris,* from Pope Paul VI in his encyclical *Populorum Progressio,* and from Vatican II in its pastoral constitution *Gaudium et Spes.*

While these papal statements have been the "headline-grabbers," other pronouncements have often been overlooked. To cite but a few instances, we may mention the encyclical letter of Leo XIII *Graves de Communi Re* (1901), Pius X's letter *Mentre Ci* (1903) and his motu proprio *Fin Dalla Prima* (1903), as well as his later encyclical epistle *Singulari Quadam* (1912), Benedict XV's letter *Soliti Nos* (1920), and Pius XII's 1941 Pentecost radio address commemorating the 50th anniversary of *Rerum Novarum* as well as his 1953 address *Colori e Quali.* All of these have supported and developed the principles of *Rerum Novarum.* Briefly, over the past 80 years there has been an unbroken string of papal pronouncements advocating social justice and the rights of the working man.

Given such a concatenation of papal pronouncements, it would seem eminently reasonable that philosophical and theological courses regarding such matters would have been welcomed with open arms. Yet the contrary seems to have been true, since some professors were regarded as "radicals" or "communists." Looking at this in a wider context, one encounters further problems.

To some theologians, this continuity of papal teaching has been the supreme irony of the entire *Humanae Vitae* situation regarding birth control. On the one hand, they see frequently repeated papal teaching both about the rights of the worker and about the grave evil of war being either openly flaunted or conveniently ignored. On the other hand, they see papal teaching about contraception being enforced with all possible vigor. Theologians themselves are confused. We are all confused. And discussion continues.

The need for the church to proclaim the gospel in terms of the social needs of man was emphasized by Pope John XXIII when, in announcing that he intended to convoke Vatican Council II, he stated:

> It is a question in fact of bringing the modern world into contact with the vivifying and perennial energies of the gospel. . . . This supernatural order must also reflect its efficiency in the other order, the temporal one, which on so many occasions is unfortunately ultimately the only one that occupies and worries men (*Humanae Salutis,* Dec. 25, 1961).

Even in the conciliar process itself there were misgivings. Should the church speak out on matters of political import? From the documents prepared by the original preparatory commissions, only one out of the 70 *schemata* (No. 7) was devoted to social order, even though two commissions (the Theological Commission and the Commission for the Apostolate of the Laity) had been concerned with this question. Schema 7 became Schema 17, and then the celebrated "Schema 13."

When finally enacted, this document spoke to the world about social and economic injustice. Although some have criticized it for being vague, it is our opinion that it represents a major advance over previous conciliar decrees. This document states and clarifies official church stances regarding war and peace, and the relationship between church and society.

"POLITICAL THEOLOGY"

Although not strictly postconciliar, this development involves a continental European theologian whose name is perhaps less well-known than those of Rahner, Küng, and de Lubac. Johannes B. Metz has written much about "political theology." His reflections are a necessary focal point of contemporary thought.

Johannes B. Metz. To many Americans, the term "political theology" sounds rather ominous, perhaps conjuring up images of smoke-filled rooms and compromises of principle. Metz, however, tries to dispel such misunderstandings by warning his readers that "political theology" does not mean an interference by the church in the just operations of the state. Thus, it is not to be confused with similar usages employed by the ancient Romans and the Stoics where "political theology" was used to justify a primacy of politics and the state's "absolute" claims. Nor should it be confused with such later usages as those employed by Machiavelli or the nineteenth-century French traditionalists who wished to restore the *ancien régime.* Furthermore, it is not to be confused with some notion of "applied theology." Briefly, political theology is *not* theology "dabbling in politics." Nor is it the church and theology being "saddled as it were unwittingly with this or that political ideology" (*Sacramentum Verbi,* V, 34 ff).

Metz himself, although his interpretation still remains unclear to this reader, probably describes political theology best:

> Political theology seeks to make contemporary theologians aware that a trial is pending between the eschatological message of Jesus and the sociopolitical reality. It insists on the permanent relation to the world inherent in the salvation merited by Jesus, a relation not to be understood in a natural-cosmological but in a social-political sense: that is, as a critical, liberating force in regard to the social world and its historical process (*Theology of Renewal,* vol. 2, p. 261).

Hans Küng. Let us also consider the writings of Hans Küng who constantly repeats that the church must always realize her social teachings as Christ-centered and present them in the light of the gospel message. Such teachings, Küng asserts, should never allow the church to become identified with any political movement. Regarding this purely religious mission of the church, Küng notes:

> The church in these last days must under no circumstances present itself as a religio-political theocracy. Its role is the spiritual *diakonia.* . . . How could it ally itself with the powers

of this world, or identify itself with any secular unit, political party, cultural organization, economic or social pressure group, or give uncritical and unqualified support to a particular economic, social, cultural, political, philosophical or ideological system? (*The Church*, p. 99)

In Küng's view, therefore, the church must in political and social issues retain its prophetic independence, constantly preaching Christ and the gospel and attempting to evaluate political, economic, and social movements in the light of Christ's teaching.

To some reactionaries, Küng's words have been disturbing. To them Küng seems to be denying the church's role as "bulwark of the political establishment." To radicals these same words are equally disturbing; to them, Küng seems to be asserting that violent revolution is uncalled-for.

Clergy and religious will continue to be involved in demonstrating and in organizing. In the light of Vatican II, such participation is at least ponderable and not totally unthinkable.

Chapter 8

WAR AND PEACE

THERE has been a significant change in Roman Catholic teaching about conscientious objectors. To understand this change fully, we must step back into history and view the development of doctrine in the making. We shall look first at the Bible, then at the early fathers of the church, then at later systematic developments of the earlier teaching, and finally at contemporary changes.

HISTORICAL BACKGROUND

In general the Old Testament's message was quite "hawkish." Yahweh himself is called a warrior (Ex. 15:3; Ps. 24:8); Yahweh fights on behalf of Israel (Ex. 14:14; Dt. 1:30 and 32:41; Jos. 10:14, 42; 23:10; 24:12; Jgs. 5:23). One could go on and on, citing divine intervention; the drowning of Pharaoh and his armies in the Red Sea and causing time to stand still at Jericho.

The teaching of the New Testament concerning war differs only slightly from that of the Old. Christ deals with a centurion as with any other person (Mt. 8:5–13; Lk. 7:2–10). Military terminology is used in apostolic letters (Eph. 6:14–17; 1 Th. 5:8). Christ himself is depicted as bringing not peace but a sword (Mt. 10:34–36). Some New Testament exegetes have interpreted this as indicating that the early Christian community expected the second coming of Christ to be so imminent that they simply did not have time to be concerned about current social problems. Thus one should not interpret the Pauline dictum, "Slaves, be subject to your masters," as a political endorsement of slavery. It was just that there was not enough time to enter into those far-reaching and ever-present problems. In speaking of the New Testament's attitude toward war, John McKenzie puts it well in observing that "since the early Christian community was not a political society and had no part in determining policy, the question did not arise as it did for the prophets" (*Dictionary of the Bible,* p. 921).

The early fathers convey a rather mixed message. It seems that many of them were opposed to Christian military service, but the reasons adduced are not really clear. Some seem to oppose Christian military service simply on the grounds that such service would require the Christian soldier to offer sacrifice to pagan gods. Others seem to oppose Christian military service on the grounds that the Christian soldier might be called upon to persecute other practicing Christians. Still others oppose Christian military service on the grounds that war is in itself evil and opposed to the Christian gospel. At any rate, the early patristic message is unclear.

The later patristic message, however, has great significance. After the Council of Nicaea, St. Augustine, bishop of Hippo in North Africa, formulated the so-called just war theory which has dominated western thinking ever since. His reasoning is logical and cannot be lightly dismissed. According to the theory of the just war, one must conclude that, in general, war is unjust; however, certain circumstances may render a particular war just.

The conditions of the just war theory are the following:

1. The war must be declared by supreme legitimate authority. Thus, it cannot be merely a dispute between parties in an individual state.
2. The war must be fought for a just cause—for instance, in de-

fense of one's country against the attack of an unjust aggressor. But even then war should be waged only as an absolutely last resort.
3. The war itself should be waged in an "appropriate" manner in such a way that it would not produce greater harm than the harm which it is seeking to avoid or correct. Similarly, soldiers must not use unjust means of warring, such as the direct killing of innocent persons.

Although the statement of these conditions may vary slightly from time to time, the Augustinian just war theory has been substantially accepted by all of the major Christian churches for the past 1500 years. During the Crusades the idea of the "just" war was transformed into the notion of the "holy" war, one which was directly willed by God. During the Middle Ages, scholastic philosophers and theologians accepted Augustine's theory with only slight modifications. At the time of the Protestant Reformation, the major churches, both Catholic and Protestant, all adopted the just war theory and only smaller groups such as the Mennonites proclaimed themselves to be "peace churches," condemning all wars. Thus it happened that all major bodies of Christians regarded some wars as just and others as unjust. The problem for the individual believer was how to determine which was which. It was not surprising, then, that theologians attempted to set up practical guidelines for individual consciences to follow.

In attempting systematically to apply the principles of the just war theory, Roman Catholic moral and ethical theologians of the past several centuries developed an outline something like this: In any war there are three possibilities—the war is either:

1. *Certainly just,* in which case the citizen has an obligation to military service. (Since he shares in the benefits of civil society, he is obliged to protect it in a just cause.) Or the war is . . .
2. *Certainly unjust,* in which case the citizen has an obligation to refuse military service. (Since the end does not justify the means, the citizen must reject the evil means.) Or the war is . . .

3. *Doubtfully just-unjust,* in which case the citizen is obliged to military service. (Since the state has access to fuller and more accurate information, the presumption of justice stands in favor of the state.)

It is essential to note that in practice only this third possibility was considered to be real. Who could possibly judge the morality of a given war? Only the state, it was argued, since only the state had adequate information. Thus it was during the First and Second World Wars that German, Italian, French, and American Roman Catholic soldiers could fight with and kill each other, all with the blessings of their local churches. And thus it was that the *New Catholic Encyclopedia* (1967) could assert that for Roman Catholics conscientious objection was morally indefensible. While there were a few Roman Catholic pacifists such as the Roman Curia's Cardinal Alfredo Ottaviani and the *Catholic Worker*'s Dorothy Day, they were an insignificant minority going contrary to common Roman Catholic teaching.

DEVELOPMENT OF DOCTRINE

Over the past several years, there has been a major change in official Roman Catholic teaching about war. A variety of factors has effected this change. First of all, technology has developed tools for waging war which were undreamed of at the beginning of the Second World War. It is one thing to list conditions under which one may throw a stone at one's neighbor; quite another for shooting an arrow at him; still another for firing a rifle at him; yet another for dropping a bomb upon him; and altogether another for dropping a nuclear bomb upon him. Secondly, television has brought home the horror of war with great impact. At one time, war was fought (at least for Americans) at a comfortable distance. Now it enters our living rooms in living color via satellite. Thirdly, the Nuremberg war crimes tribunal established, as a part of international law, the principle that individuals are responsible for their acts of war, regardless of national policies or superiors' orders. Finally, there has been much deeper theological insight both into love as the central focal point of Christianity and conscience as the responsibility of the individual person, one which cannot be simply handed over to the state.

For the American public, we wish to single out four official church statements which reflect and indicate this change. Although Pope Pius XII condemned the excesses of modern warfare and Pope John XXIII questioned the rationality of any modern war, it is only during the reign of Pope Paul VI that the major change has occurred.

PAUL VI AT THE UNITED NATIONS. On October 4, 1965, Pope Paul VI, in an allocution to the General Assembly of the United Nations, his voice quivering with emotion, pleaded in never-to-be-forgotten words: "No more war. War never again!" Both earlier and subsequent official pronouncements by Pope Paul afford clear theological evidence that this was not merely a public humanitarian gesture, but rather a public exercise of papal teaching authority which cannot be lightly dismissed.

THE SECOND VATICAN COUNCIL. December 7, 1965 marked the formal promulgation of the Second Vatican Council's Pastoral Constitution on the "Church in the Modern World." This remarkable pastoral document in its fifth chapter (Introduction and Section I, articles 77–82) discusses the nature of both peace and war, condemning every act of total war in very unequivocal terms: "This most holy Synod . . . issues the following declaration: Any act of war aimed indiscriminately at the destruction of entire cities or of extensive areas along with their population is a crime against God and man himself. It merits unequivocal and unhesitating condemnation" (Article 80). With regard to the pastoral constitution, two points should be specially noted. First, application of the just war theory is now limited *only* to *defensive* wars. Previously, it had applied to both offensive and defensive wars. Secondly, for the first time in official church teaching, provision is made for the conscientious objector. While these two points may seem insignificant to many readers, they are very important because they represent an official statement of an ecumenical council on a topic previously considered too delicate to handle.

U.S. BISHOPS' PASTORAL OF 1968. In November of 1968, the hierarchy of the United States of America issued a national pastoral letter on "Human Life in Our Day" which both reaffirmed the teachings of the Second Vatican Council on war and peace and also proposed a modification of the Selective Service Act allowing for "selective conscientious objection."

1969 STATEMENT. On October 15, 1969, the United States Catholic Conference's Division of World Justice and Peace issued a statement on "The Catholic Conscientious Objector." While this statement was not issued by the entire hierarchy, it was released by an official committee of the U.S. Catholic Conference and has, at the very least, the status of quasi-official church teaching. In this statement the following recommendations are made:

> a. That each diocese initiate or cooperate in providing draft information and counseling;
> b. That Catholic organizations which could qualify as alternative service agencies consider applying for that status, and support and provide meaningful employment for the conscientious objector.

1971 STATEMENT. The U.S. Bishops further clarified their position in a letter dated October 21, 1971, wherein they reviewed the teaching of Vatican II. Attempting to dispel the mistaken notion that a Catholic cannot under any circumstances be a conscientious objector, this letter very clearly and unequivocally asserts:

> In the light of the Gospel and from an analysis of the church's teaching on conscience, it is clear that a Catholic can be a conscientious objector to war in general or to a particular war "because of religious training and belief."

Moreover the bishops conclude this 1971 letter by making two specific recommendations: (1) that the Selective Service Act be modified to permit selective conscientious objectors; and (2) that peacetime conscription into military service be ended. Finally, the letter's very last paragraph urges civil officials to consider granting amnesty both to those in prison and to those who have emigrated "to be ready to serve in other ways to show that they are sincere objectors."

One notes with interest that this Declaration does not condemn those who have served in the armed forces. In fact, it repeats traditional Catholic teaching described above: "The church has traditionally upheld the obligation of Christians to serve in military defensive forces. . . . Such community oriented service . . . has merited the church's commendation." There is no contradiction here, for the bishops are merely repeating Vatican II's plea that a choice be made available.

CONCLUSION

From the Bible to Saint Augustine, from the Crusades to the Reformation, from Thomas Aquinas to the Second Vatican Council to today, what are the most significant changes in Catholic teaching about war and peace? I suggest that they are two in number:

> 1. In official Roman Catholic teaching the just war theory is still valid, but only in regard to *limited defensive* wars in which no act of total war is perpetrated.

2. The Roman Catholic citizen can now be a conscientious objector. Indeed, he is *obliged* to follow his conscience. Pacifism is seen today as a charismatic vocation. Are all Catholics called to be celibate? No. Are some? Yes. Is celibacy therefore an obligation for some, but not for all? Yes. Are all Catholics called to pacifism? No. Some? Yes. Is pacifism therefore an obligation for some, but not for all? Yes.

Chapter 9

ECUMENISM

IN 1954, when the World Council of Churches held its Second International General Assembly in Evanston, Illinois, there were no official Roman Catholic representatives present. In fact, Chicago's Cardinal Samuel Stritch had issued a pastoral letter prohibiting Roman Catholic observers and forbidding priests to attend the Assembly, even as journalists. Moreover, when the predominantly Protestant World Council announced a general prayer meeting at Chicago's Soldier Field, Roman Catholics responded by proclaiming a Marian Year hour of devotion in the same Soldier Field.

However, in 1961 and again in 1968, when the World Council of Churches held its Third and Fourth International General Assemblies in New Delhi, India, and in Uppsala, Sweden, the Roman Catholic church was represented by *official* observers. There obviously has been a great change here. What has been the cause of this change?

THE NATURE OF ECUMENISM

In speaking of ecumenism, one must avoid certain excesses. First of all, by ecumenism one does not mean the forming of a new "superchurch." Thus, some members of the Jewish community have mistakenly regarded the ecumenical movement as a sort of master plan on the part of Christians to convert all Jews and, indeed, all non-Christians to Christianity. Likewise, ecumenism does not mean an erasing of all doctrinal and moral differences between church bodies.

Etymologically, the word "ecumenical" is derived from the Greek word *oikoumene,* meaning "the entire inhabited earth." In the course of time, however, this word has taken on many different meanings. Thus, scholars have described at least six such meanings: (1) belonging to or representing the Roman Empire; (2) belonging to or representing the church as a whole; (3) having general validity or meaning throughout the church; (4) concerning a worldwide mission activity of the church; (5) concerning relations between the churches or between Christians of different confessions; (6) referring both to the awareness that all churches and all Christians belong to the worldwide Christian community, and to the readiness of all Christians to work for the unity of the church of Christ.

THE BEGINNINGS OF ECUMENISM

To look at the question more practically and to understand fully the ecumenical movement and changes which have occurred therein, one must look to the movement's sources, especially its Protestant and Roman Catholic origins. Let us examine them separately.

During the nineteenth century, many efforts were made to bring about collaboration among Protestant churches. The sixteenth-century Reformation had brought about not only separation from Rome, but also division and dissension among the various protesting groups themselves. Over the course of the years, Lutherans had moved away from Presbyterians, Anglo-Catholics from Methodists and Baptists, not even to mention such "radical" reformers as the Anabaptists. Thus, the following organizations were established: the World YMCA (1855), the Christian Endeavor movement (1881), and the world YWCA (1894). At the same time two other movements were established: the Evangelical Alliance (London, 1846), and the Federal Council of Churches of Christ in the United States (1908).

In 1910 a meeting of Protestant missionaries at Edinburgh, Scotland, decided to form a more general organization of the churches. In the words of Father John B. Sheerin: "The general meeting gave rise to a movement for Christian unity that branched into two submovements—*faith and order* and *life and work*, the first to deal with theological questions and the second to deal with problems of social action." Although a decision had been reached in 1939 to form one single organization to study mutual problems and concerns, the outbreak of the Second World War postponed further action until 1948 when the World Council of Churches was born. Its first General Assembly met that year in Amsterdam, Holland.

Although some feel that Roman Catholic ecumenical involvement began with Pope John XXIII, the fact of the matter is that the real basis for such involvement was established by Pope Leo XIII. In his encyclical letter *Satis Cognitum* (1897), Pope Leo ruled that the nine days of prayer in preparation for Pentecost should be especially devoted to the intention of development of unity among Christians. On another occasion, Pope Leo asserted very strongly: "We are not unaware of the lengthy and difficult labors required for that order of things whose restoration we desire, and many will no doubt consider that we are leaving too much to hope, and pursuing an ideal more to be wished for than expected. But we put all our hope and trust in Jesus Christ, the savior of the human race, remembering the great things that the folly of the cross and its proclamation were formerly able to accomplish in the face of the wisdom of this world." Again Pope Leo wrote: "For a long time Catholics all over the world have awaited you, with the anxiousness of a brotherly love, that you might serve God with us in the unity of the same gospel, the same faith, the same hope, bound by perfect love."

During the pontificate of Pope Pius XII, however, ecumenical affairs became somewhat confused. In 1948 a decree of the Holy Office forbade Roman Catholic participation in any meetings with non-Catholics at which religion would be discussed. Shortly thereafter (December 20, 1949), the Holy Office issued a very ambiguous decree, which created mixed reactions in ecumenical circles. On the one hand it permitted bishops to foster ecumenical discussions by competent priests. But this portion of the decree pertained only to meetings sponsored by Roman Catholics.

And yet, in referring to assemblies sponsored by other churches, this same instruction (entitled *Ecclesia Catholica*) states very bluntly: "The Catholic church takes no part in ecumenical conventions and other assemblies of similar nature." Thus, in effect, this instruction has stated, on the one hand, that ecumenical meetings under Roman Catholic sponsorship were permitted. On the other hand, the very same document had stated that ecumenical discussions under Protestant sponsorship were not acceptable. It is only in this context that one can understand Cardinal Stritch's forbidding Roman Catholic participation in the World Council of Churches' 1954 General Assembly.

On June 5, 1960, Pope John XXIII established a secretariat for promoting Christian unity and appointed Cardinal Augustine Bea as its head. On December 5, 1960, Pope John received a courtesy visit from the Archbishop of Canterbury. In 1961 the Vatican sent five official observers to the World Council of Churches General Assembly at New Delhi, India; a short time later, on October 11, 1962, Pope John addressed the opening meeting of the Second Vatican Council.

That same council, at its third general session (1964), approved the document on ecumenism and in it urged bishops all over the world to promote Christian unity. As Father Sheerin observes: "The approval of this document as well as the presence of Protestant observers at the council has resulted in closer ecumenical ties between the Catholic church and the World Council of Churches, climaxed by the visit of Cardinal Bea to the World Council of Churches headquarters in Geneva on February 18, 1965. There he formally accepted the World Council's invitation to appoint six Catholic experts to join eight World Council experts on a committee to explore the prospects and possibilities of dialogue between the Catholic church and the World Council of Churches."

GETTING IT TOGETHER

From the Roman Catholic point of view, this change can be understood only in the context of St. Robert Bellarmine's teaching about the nature of the church. As we have seen, Bellarmine regarded the church as a visible structure. One was either within this structure or one was outside of it. We have already mentioned (cf. Chapter 1) how Pope Pius XII in 1943 had repeated Bellarmine's position about membership in the church.

In his encyclical letter *Humani Generis* (1950), Pope Pius XII carried Bellarmine's teaching even further. The Pope explicitly condemned those who "through an imprudent zeal for souls are urged by a great inherent desire to do away with the barrier that divides good and honest men. These advocate an 'irenism' according to which, by setting aside the questions which divide men, they aim not only at joining forces to repel the attacks of atheism, but also at reconciling things opposed to one another in the field of dogma" (Number 12). Furthermore, Pope Pius specifically condemned such an opinion, writing: "But some, through enthusiasm for an imprudent irenism, seem to consider as an obstacle to the restoration of fraternal union the things founded on the laws and principles given by Christ and likewise on institutions founded by him; for these are the defense and support of the integrity of the faith, the removal of which would bring about the union of all, but only to their destruction."

It is not surprising, then, that one finds in this period little Roman Catholic inclination toward the ecumenical movement. The Roman Catholic church was the church of Christ, and no other church was. To talk about relating to other churches was, in that framework, quite unthinkable. In fact, official Roman Catholic church documents customarily did not even use the term "church" in describing these other Christian communities.

And so it was that this era of tension endured. Both sides demanded total capitulation from each other. Roman Catholics demanded that Protestants return as a whole to the Roman Catholic church. Protestants in turn demanded that Roman Catholics repudiate all their claims and join them on an equal basis. Perhaps the best brief summary of this problem is found in the words of Hans Küng: "Precisely because they were once one community, a single unity, the breach made such a deep and lasting impact. What happened was not a quarrel between two strangers, but a division and opposition of flesh and blood—a wound which time alone will not heal" (*The Church*, p. 308).

ECUMENISM TODAY?

What has happened to the ecumenical movement today? During the mid-1960s, as we have seen, ecumenism seemed to be flourishing, but at present it seems to be suffering from some sort of *malaise*. How can one explain this?

Jesuit theologian Walter J. Burghardt attributes ecumenical difficulties to three problems—suspicion, impatience, and inertia. Regarding suspicion, he notes that there are some, both Protestant and Catholic, who suspect that ecumenism is a subtle sellout. These see Catholicism being Protestantized and Protestantism Catholicized. Impatience, he continues, plagues both Catholics and Protestants who feel that the ecumenical movement is dragging its heels. These see an incongruity in Catholics and Protestants admitting a common possession of Christ and the Spirit and yet refusing to go further in sharing this common possession. Related to this is the third problem, inertia. Many Catholics and Protestants have experienced a crisis of rising expectations in that the enthusiastic glow of the 1960s seems to be bogged down by a mass of bureaucratic red tape and structural problems.

I suggest that the problems mentioned by Burghardt are very real, but that their solution is found in a rather unlikely place. Structurally, the ecumenical movement moves along steadily—at a pace which may disconcert some. Catholics and Protestants do continue to work together in the World Council of Churches, the National Council of Churches, and various regional and local organizations.

Theologically, collaboration and dialogue also continue among Catholic and Protestant scholars. Here in the United States the recently established Council on the Study of Religion provides a sort of "umbrella group" for major Catholic and Protestant scholarly organizations. The recent international congress of scholars and theologians held in Los Angeles is also a sign of vitality on this level. Moreover, the new joint Roman Catholic-Lutheran theological statement on the Eucharist and also the "ecumenical consensus" statement sponsored by the National Council of Churches offer concrete evidence of progress.

The heart of the ecumenical problem today is found, I feel, in an ever-increasing "polarization" within the churches themselves. One may describe this polarization in a variety of ways. The Rev. Dr. Graydon Snyder states his opinion that real eucharistic division lies between what he calls "strong free-church" and "strong Lutheran" positions. Others have described polarization in terms of "faith theology" as opposed to "work theology." Moreover, others speak in terms of a "pietist-pragmatist" split; still others, in terms of a "reactionary-radical" division.

Dr. George Docherty, a Presbyterian from New York, wryly notes: "It is ironic that at a time when divisive ecclesiastical barriers are being broken down, the whole nature and purpose of the church's mission should be hotly and costingly called into question inside its own fellowship."

In other words, the entire ecumenical movement has shifted its major point of emphasis. Resolution of today's problems will depend on the churches' ability to recognize and cope with this shift.

Chapter 10

RELIGIOUS LIFE

ONLY ten years ago, nuns, brothers and priests were easily recognized in public places—they wore religious habits or black suits with distinctive neck and sometimes headgear. Convents, rectories, and monasteries were quiet places of retreat where the "religious" man or woman lived and often worked. Yet today we hear of and often see nuns wearing ordinary dresses without veils, brothers and priests wearing neckties, and religious living in apartments or houses away from their former quiet retreats. What changes have occurred here? Has religious life lost its former meaning?

INTRODUCTORY COMMENTS

Let us note at the outset that "religious life" has, from very early times, had a specific technical meaning—a life consecrated to God, seeking assimilation of Christ's redemptive acts through a vowed observance of the evangelical counsels of poverty, chastity, and obedience. However, there have frequently been many misunderstandings. Religious life does not necessarily involve communal living; there have been religious houses with as few as one or two persons. Religious life does not necessarily involve a peculiar clothing-style, which has varied from place to place and time to time. Nor does religious life necessarily involve a particular type of work; there have been hospital workers, both men and women as well as lay and religious; and there have been religious-order parish priests as well as diocesan priest-teachers.

All of these—communal living, clothing style, type of apostolic work—are quite accidental to religious life as such, which derives its essential distinguishing mark from the profession of the three vows. To put it in another way, one frequently hears of a distinction between "clergy," "religious," and "laity," as though these were three completely separate groups within the church. Such a tripartite division is not quite accurate. Actually, there are two separate distinctions which must be made. One is between clergy and laity and is based upon a choice of ordained ministerial service to the community. The other is between religious and laity and is based upon one's choice of means in striving for perfection—whether through the vows or not. It is for this reason that the diocesan clergy has frequently been called the "secular" clergy (as distinguished from "religious" clergy).

The taking of religious vows (or "profession") has traditionally been divided into temporary (for a trial period of one or more years) and final, which in turn could be either simple or solemn profession, depending upon the particular religious order.

HISTORICAL ORIGINS OF RELIGIOUS LIFE

There have been significant changes in religious life in today's church. Let us proceed to examine them more closely.

The "evangelical counsels" of poverty, chastity, and obedience surely have a New Testament foundation. Regarding poverty, many fathers dwelled upon the rich young man who was advised to sell his possessions and follow Christ (Mt. 19:16–22; Mk. 10:17–22; Lk. 18:18–23). But many others emphasized 2 Cor. 8:9—"Remember how generous the Lord Jesus was: he was rich, but he

became poor for your sake, to make you rich out of his poverty."
Regarding chastity, most authors referred to 1 Cor. 7:32–34:

> An unmarried man can devote himself to the Lord's affairs;
> all he need worry about is pleasing the Lord; but a married
> man has to bother about the world's affairs and devote him-
> self to pleasing his wife: he is torn two ways. In the same
> way an unmarried woman, like a young girl, can devote her-
> self to the Lord's affairs; all she need worry about is being
> holy in body and spirit. The married woman, on the other
> hand, has to worry about the world's affairs and devote her-
> self to pleasing her husband.

Regarding obedience, many referred to Mt. 26:39—" 'My Father,'
he said, 'if it is possible, let this cup pass me by. Nevertheless, let
it be as you, not I, would have it.' "

As we have already seen, certain early Christians retreated
from the "world" and retired to the desert in order to achieve a
more perfect "spiritual" encounter with God. The precise beginning of religious life, in the sense of the date when professing
three vows became required, is rather obscure. At first, such persons led the lives of hermits in a rather solitary fashion, but
gradually they tended to form into settlements or communities.
Although the precise beginning of religious life in the sense of
the three vows is still rather obscure, some feel that this practice
was first introduced by St. Pachomius in Egypt around A.D. 325.
Somewhat later (380), Basil the Great opposed the notion of total
separation from the world, asserting that in such isolation one
could not completely observe the mandate to love one's neighbor.

The next major step in the development of western religious
orders was the spread of Benedictine monasticism. In fact, the
Rule of St. Benedict has become a classic and continues today to
exercise great influence. Toward the early part of the sixth century, Benedict, who had led a hermit's life near Subiaco, founded
a monastery at Monte Cassino, where he stayed for the rest of

his life. Although some think that he did this in rejection of the hermitical lifestyle, others are convinced that he founded the monastery because he was forced to do so by large numbers of disciples. This later view seems more likely.

As Abbé Jacques Winandy of Clairvaux once noted, Benedict borrowed most of his observance from Eastern monasticism— community of goods, poverty of clothing, exact obedience, silence in the Abbot's presence, division of the community into deaneries, number of psalms in the night office, the three occupations at stated times in the day (prayer, sacred reading, manual labor), brevity of silent prayer in choir, perpetual abstinence from meat, broad and generous hospitality, and a retreat far from the world and all its noise (*Some Schools of Catholic Spirituality*, p. 22).

While monasticism developed, there also grew up a series of abuses, with the result that many other monastic groups were formed, such as the Cistercians, who wished to return to a strict observance of Benedict's Rule in a very literal interpretation. At the time of the Crusades, other communities emerged with the intentions of waging war with the heathen and caring for pilgrims.

The beginning of the 13th century marked the formation of the Franciscan, Carmelite, and Dominican orders—the so-called mendicant orders. (The formation of the Carmelites remains somewhat obscure. Some assert that they were founded by the prophet Elias at Mount Carmel; generally, however, 1155 is considered the date of their foundation, when St. Berthold established a hermitage on Mount Carmel.) In the following years, numerous arguments occurred about the "correct" and proper interpretation of each group's rules. Thus, there developed groups of "regulars," "spirituals," "conventuals," "strict observers," and so forth.

The year 1534 (in the midst of the Reformation) marked the formation of the Society of Jesus. Saint Ignatius Loyola and his six companions seem to have started with a rather limited objective—that of evangelizing the heathen in the Holy Land—but when this proved impractical, their objective became much more general in that the society was placed at the disposition of the pope. In fact, "professed" members of the society took a fourth vow—one of special obedience to the pope. (Such a fourth vow was not a novelty, since the Benedictines have long taken a vow of "stability" to remain in one monastery.)

After the Reformation, religious societies or "congregations" multiplied rapidly—for the care of the sick, the education of orphans, the education of children, and so on. Space prevents mention of all such groups, each with its own identity. As we shall see shortly, this multiplication has led to serious problems about religious life today.

Religious orders, both older and newer, have two fundamental documents directing their life and activities—their Constitution and their Rule. For canonical or legal approval, each order must have these documents approved by Rome (Congregation for Religious). While the Rule usually deals with more practical, specific details of activity, the Constitution is a more general statement of principles underlying the order's entire life and work. The Constitution generally begins with a twofold statement of the order's purpose, ordinarily stating the primary purpose as the sanctification of its members through the three vows and giving as secondary purpose the order's principal occupation (e.g., missionary or hospital work, teaching, etc.). Orders were generally distinguished in their secondary purpose between "active" and "contemplative."

THE CURRENT SCENE

The Second Vatican Council issued a specific "Decree on the Appropriate Renewal of Religious Life." Some have criticized this decree for being too closely related to older manuals of ascetics. Others have criticized it for relying too heavily on religious priests, thereby seeming not to give appropriate voice either to nuns or to brothers. Most, however, admit that the decree is at the very least a step in the right direction.

The very title is somewhat significant. It speaks of "renewal" not simply in terms of a return to or restoration of early monastic rules, but rather in terms of "appropriate" renewal, i.e., one accommodated to modern times. This twofold theme recurs frequently throughout the decree.

We mention only briefly and in passing the Council's continued approval of "secular institutes," first officially approved by Pope Pius XII in 1947. Such institutes differ from religious life in that there is no public profession of vows and community living is not required.

Speaking specifically about renewal of religious life, the Council Fathers mention two necessarily spontaneous processes—a "return to the sources" and an adjustment of the community to modern times. They then detail five specifics:

1. The following of Christ as proposed by the Gospel is to be regarded as the "supreme law" of all communities.
2. Loyal recognition should be given to the communities' founders and their spirit, as well as to the heritage of each community.
3. Each community should participate in the life of the church in its own way—whether this concerns "scriptural, liturgical, doctrinal, pastoral, ecumenical, missionary, or social" matters.
4. Communities should "promote among their members a suitable awareness of contemporary human conditions and of the needs of the church."
5. Communities must not forget that the central need is that of a renewal of spirit which prompts them "to an imitation of Christ and to union with God through the profession of the evangelical counsels." They conclude: "Such an interior renewal must always be accorded the leading role even in the promotion of exterior works" (*Perfectae Caritatis*, #2).

With regard to the three essential vows themselves, Vatican II offered several valuable insights. While insisting upon the three vows, the Council Fathers noted:

1. Re *Poverty:* Depending on the circumstances of their location, communities as such should aim at giving a kind of
corporate witness to their own poverty. Let them willingly
contribute something from their own resources to the
other needs of the church and to the support of the poor.
. . . To the degree that their rules and constitutions permit, religious communities can rightly possess whatever is
necessary for their temporal life and mission. Still, let
them avoid every appearance of luxury, of excessive
wealth, and accumulation of possessions.
2. Re *Chastity:* Above all, everyone should remember—superiors especially—that chastity has stronger safeguards in
a community when true fraternal love thrives among its
members.
3. Re *Obedience:* Let chapters and councils faithfully acquit
themselves of the governing role given to them; each
should express in its own way the fact that all members of
the community have a share in the welfare of the whole
community and a responsibility for it (*Perfectae Caritatis,*
#12–14).

In other words, while earlier traditional manuals of ascetical
theology had treated the vows in a somewhat negative manner,
the bishops at Vatican II restated the purpose of vows in a positive way.

In the period following Vatican II, religious communities
faced some very serious difficulties occasioned not only by the
Council's call for renewal, but also by the more general phenomenon of world change. Adrian Hastings points out five such difficulties in his *Guide to the Documents of Vatican II,* vol. 2, pp.
186–7:

1. The recent proliferation of new societies has not been accom-
panied by a decrease in the older groups, even when the purpose for their founding has ceased to exist.
2. There has been an increasingly deep difference in emphasis
between older "flight from the world" spiritualities and con-

temporary spiritualities demanding participation in the world's culture. This is vaguely reminiscent of Basil the Great.

3. Vatican II, in emphasizing the *universal* call to holiness, reminded Roman Catholics that such a call was not restricted only to the religious life.

4. Over the centuries there developed an unfounded confusion between "monastic" lifestyles and those of religious. Hastings asks: "Can anything be really more different than the life, vocation and mission of a Carthusian monk and a missionary nursing sister? Yet they are in the same juridical category—"religious with vows." We remind our readers that we had spoken earlier of how the origins of religious life began with the hermits, then spread to monasteries, which became the classic models of spirituality. Frequently, then, such a monastic lifestyle was imposed not only upon nonmonastic religious, but also upon diocesan priests and seminarians.

5. Religious communities of women face specific problems over and above the preceding in that many of their Constitutions and Rules were formulated before the proper recognition of the role of women in the church.

To these we add two observations of our own. The first is related to Hastings' first point. Many have criticized duplication of efforts among religious communities. Others, though, have noted that such duplication stems not so much from petty jealousy, but rather from an insufficient rethinking of the community's purpose. If one has four separate communities aimed at education "of orphans," "of children," "of young women," and "of young men"; moreover, if one has four separate communities for the care "of the sick," "of the poor," "of the aging," and "of the alcoholic"; and if one finds five missionary communities working among "the American Indian," "the Asian Indian," "the Moslem," "the American Black," and "the African Black," it is small wonder that all this overlapping causes an identity crisis among religious orders.

Our second observation deals with "recruiting practices." The major criticism has been that "vocational directors" have frequently become "recruiting agents." Tragic results have occurred —the "perfect" diocesan priest candidate dropping out of the Dominicans, the "ideal" B.V.M. candidate dropping out of the Benedictines. There has been some progress here, but much remains to be done before the vocational director is seen not as a recruiter, but as a counselor enabling candidates to choose from among a wide variety of available opinions.

Changes will continue to occur in religious life. They may seem distressing, but changes from a hermit's life to the monastery community undoubtedly were equally distressing at one time. Again, the very fact of change is a sign of life and vitality.